The Invitation

THE
Invitation

~

CLIFTON TAULBERT

NEWSOUTH BOOKS

Montgomery

NewSouth Books
105 S. Court Street
Montgomery, AL 36104

Library of Congress Cataloging-in-Publication Data available upon request.
ISBN 978-1-58838-307-5 (hardcover)
ISBN 978-1-60306-351-7 (ebook)

Design by Randall Williams
Printed in the United States of America
by Maple Press

To my son,
MARSHALL DANZY TAULBERT,
and to his generation of Americans
and those who will follow.

We baby boomers were once considered the Generation of Promise—the generation to remodel America as we passed through it. Much remains to be done. Those who follow us must take up the gauntlet and become the new Generations of Promise—the Americans who through their daily living will do their part to move us closer to the ideals of a shared democracy and creating lingering lessons worthy of remembrance.

To the Generations of Promise:

Remember to be gentle with yourself and others. We are all children of chance, and none can say why some fields will blossom while others lay brown beneath the August sun. Care for those around you. Look past your differences. Their dreams are no less than yours, their choices in life no more easily made.

And give. Give in any way you can, of whatever you possess. To give is to love. To withhold is to wither. Care less for your harvest than for how it is shared, and your life will have meaning and your heart will have peace.

— KENT NERBURN

Contents

Preface

As an African American born in the Mississippi Delta during legal segregation, I feel forever conflicted. The South is this eternal place I love, the place where I first saw the sun and admired the moon, where I first laughed and cried. It was the place where I first heard music with no idea of how important it would be to the rest of my life. My elders called music "the voice of our souls." They were so right. Whether I was happy or sad, music would provide solace and follow me for the rest of my life. As it often was for my elders, music also became my safe conversation—the sounds of my soul that others could hear and join in, or the soulful humming that only I could hear. From my small Glen Allan, Mississippi, hometown to worlds beyond great bodies of water, I have never been without the voice of my soul.

Yes, the South, my eternal place, was also the first place I heard my own voice and the voices of others—those who loved me and those who sought to define my life by the color of my skin. Skin color would be the "forever" branding that would bring into our lives the multiple lessons of race and place required for our survival, lessons that often evoked the music from our souls, becoming the conversations we wanted to hold.

Yes, the music was there . . . in this eternal place where I would grow up loving the people who loved me, and loving the food we shared and the good memories we made together. At the same time, and in the same place, I grew up dreaming of a better place, simply because of how I had to live whenever I stepped outside the homes that were ours. I was not one of "them," the landed gentry who set in motion a way of life for those who looked like me—a way of living that had evolved out of slavery and dared the Emancipation to change it. During my childhood years, legal segregation was my world; hence the required lessons of survival—lessons that many might assume would have fallen by the wayside as the decades passed and progressive education and monumental social legislation came into our lives. However, for me and so many other African American baby boomers, this would not be the case. Despite all that moved us forward, those powerful and defining lessons have had such a tenacious hold that they continue to surface.

This reality was not lost on me. During my life, long after leaving the Delta, lessons I had been taught and experiences I had as a child continued to impact my thinking and even today keep me second-guessing the world of "them" that surrounds me. I have gone very few days without some reference to the presence in my life of those lingering lessons of race and place.

AT THE TURN OF the millennium, however, I was privileged to deliver a speech in Philadelphia, Pennsylvania, for the annual Character Education Conference. My speech was actually a conversation about the importance of building community and the principles required to do so. Apparently it resonated with the audience, which included several delegates from South Carolina who subsequently invited me to speak in their state.

The South Carolinians' invitations were extended several times over a five-year period. During those five years, I had experiences that seemed to have been orchestrated beyond my control. I found myself on a seesaw, intimidated and inspired, as well as anxious and excited, and repeatedly dissecting the world of "them" and "us."

Eventually I went to Allendale, South Carolina, to deliver a speech on the power of community. On that occasion, and during follow-up visits,

I experienced a surreal feeling that my childhood persona—that familiar and cautious voice from my segregated childhood that I affectionately call Little Cliff—was emerging. With every step, I could sense familiar emotions from my small cotton community escalating. I could feel this internal tugging between the adult I had become and the lessons of my youth that still shadowed me. It was unplanned and unexpected, but powerful nonetheless. Both Little Cliff and the man I had become would make unexpected discoveries while in Allendale.

Some of those times, I felt completely vulnerable and isolated, despite how progressive my personal journey had been professionally. Little Cliff, the voice of my past, was admonishing me not to throw caution to the wind. He had memories that I had held close to my chest. When I was a teenager I had believed that the much-talked-about integration and federal intervention would immediately bring about the equality that our songs demanded. Soon, I was sure, my color would no longer be considered a badge of dishonor. I waited. It didn't happen. I tried to forget that disappointment, but Little Cliff never forgot. As much as I wanted to embrace change and remain unhampered by past lessons, Little Cliff called for caution.

Unable to let others in on those personal feelings—or choosing not to—I found myself doing as my elders had, relying on the voice of my soul, allowing the words of songs to walk me through all that I was feeling and to hold me steady. It was not unusual to hear comforting songs, long since forgotten by most, still ringing in my ears. No one else could hear Sam Cooke's voice reminding me that *a change was gonna come,* but I would hum along, alone. I wanted to believe the words from Sam Cooke's soul. They sounded so hopeful at a time when hope was mostly all we had. As an adult, I was walking in some of that change. I knew this. But Little Cliff, the cautious little boy who walks beside me daily, was still in search of that complete change he was promised so long ago.

The far-reaching and tenacious lessons of race and place that shadow my life grew out of hundreds of years of slavery and segregation in America. I still recall as a young boy going uptown with my Great-Aunt Elna and being outside our public library, looking in through the window that fronted the sidewalk, but unable to check out the book I desperately wanted to read.

"You can't go in there."

I can still see my great-aunt brushing my creative desire away while tightly holding my hand, and another gentle lesson of race and place was taught and learned. At an early and formative age, I had to forgo my natural inclinations and learn how to maneuver in the world of "them" and "us." In such a world, it was necessary for my elders to embrace the songs of our people that were the voices of our souls, and I found it so for me as well.

My experiences in Allendale would bring back all these memories from my childhood in the Mississippi Delta. Like our remembered music, they would reach deeply into my soul.

By the winter of 2006, my work in Allendale had come to an end, but my personal experiences remained fresh in my mind. It was a time to reflect on all that had transpired. I sat at my kitchen table and began collecting my thoughts about this surreal community I had become a part of in South Carolina. I was still somewhat in disbelief of what I had experienced. I would quietly rifle through years of memories and incidents that I had collected in notes. I found myself talking with friends who had worked in South Carolina along with me. I needed their memories to balance my own. What I had encountered there had a visceral impact upon me, but I also knew my experiences to be universal. They reminded me of the need to start afresh—to engage in "people-to-people" conversations around the subject of race and place, the kind of conversations that former President Bill Clinton initiated in the 1990s with the help of the noted African American historian Dr. John Hope Franklin (now deceased). I knew I had to write about my Allendale experience.

As you walk with me through these fifteen chapters, I want you to be

reminded of the "beloved community" so eloquently described by Dr. Martin
Luther King—somewhat like the community of integration I dreamed of as
a boy. I want you to understand what it takes to build such a heroic place
and how easy it is to allow ourselves to fall into a way of living that can
become suffocating to others, leaving them forever on the outside looking
in, wondering if the change promised by Sam Cooke would come in their
lifetime. It is my wish that baby boomers of all races might find themselves
in this story. Hopefully, we can come away energized and committed to do
more to fix that which is broken. Maybe we can pass along to the generations that follow a much clearer picture of what America can be and what is
required of each of us. We must challenge our children and grandchildren to
become like Fats Domino—who created transformative music that reached
far beyond New Orleans—extending an invitation for all to sit at his table.

My personal experience in Allendale, South Carolina, turned out to be
just such a challenging and transformative time for me, taking me beyond
where I had been and into a place I could not have imagined as a child. The
intense personal experiences that I had there were unprecedented, unforget-
table, unexpected, and surprising at every turn. Because of what happened
to me in Allendale, I know we can create a past worth remembering—one
that celebrates the best of who we are and who we can become.

I never expected the invitation to Allendale, nor what happened to me
and for me there. In spite of my hesitation and the pain of my segregated
childhood that resurfaced as a result, the invitation turned out to be worth
accepting. It was an invitation to a journey I needed to take. This is your
invitation. Please join me.

ACKNOWLEDGMENTS

I would not have been able to complete this memoir if not for my wife,
Barbara. She graciously provided me the time and the emotional energy
needed to take on this project in 2006 and to stay with it. Going back and

remembering things you really want to forget can be painful. Sometimes while writing, I just wanted to be left alone. The memories were all too real, but that made it even more important that I share them with others. Hopefully, Barbara understood.

The Invitation provided my first opportunity to meet Beth Lieberman, a New York publishing house editor and student rabbi, who coaxed out of me more than I imagined could be done. I took her to a world that for her had been in books, but for me was my life. Beth, thank you for being one of my editors, and for not only bringing your expertise to the project, but also your personal sensitivity to what I am trying to accomplish with this memoir—a place to start a meaningful conversation on race and place and the lingering impact of those harsh and gentle lessons.

Professor Nancy Grisham Anderson, thank you for being my line editor, helping me to pause where I should. Thank you for your friendship over the years and for being the fellow Southerner who clearly understands my journey. I also want to thank Dr. Sally Dennison, who is having the last look at this literary journey. Dr. Dennison edited my very first book, *Once Upon a Time When We Were Colored*—the award-winning book that set me on this incredible writing journey. More than any other editor, she knows my heart and what I'm trying to accomplish as a writer. I am so glad she found time to join me on this journey.

And lastly, I want to thank Douglas Decker, who works with me, for reading this manuscript from the start in 2006 and living through all the title changes.

Special thanks to the many people who have chosen to read what I have written and continue to ask me for more. This is the more you requested.

⁓

The Invitation

1

Public Observations, Private Conversations

"We are very much what others think of us. The reception our observations meet with gives us courage to proceed, or damps our efforts." —William Hazlitt

THE INVITATION CAME IN 2000 IN PHILADELPHIA, PENNSYL-vania, where I was delivering a keynote address at an international character education conference. I was excited to be one of the speakers and equally excited to be back in this grand historic city for only the second time in my life.

As a young boy growing up in Glen Allan, Mississippi, I had loved Philadelphia from a distance due to the lively and colorful conversations I heard between Cousin Lula Harris and Mama Ponk, my great-aunt who raised me. Becoming a writer had allowed me to fulfill a childhood dream—visiting Cousin Lula's Philadelphia. My first visit in 1989 was to celebrate the publication of my book *Once Upon a Time When We Were Colored*. Philadelphia's Free Library had extended the invitation and I still get goosebumps when I think of that visit and how I felt as a new writer. A child of "colored" field hands and maids in a little town in the Mississippi Delta, I had grown up, gone north, gotten an education, and written the aforementioned book about my childhood. The book had been recognized in the pages of *Publishers Weekly.*

This second visit was different. I was not the novice writer celebrating his first book. This time I was coming as a seasoned writer with four additional published books, including *The Last Train North*, which was nominated for the Pulitzer Prize, and *The Eight Habits of the Heart*, which was recognized by *USA Today* as their year-end "Book to Build Our Lives" and had garnered my invitation to speak at the character education conference.

More than anyone else could understand, I knew that speaking at this conference was beyond the dreams of my youth. Even when I heard Cousin Lula and Mama Ponk talking about this faraway Philadelphia, I never dreamed it to be a place I would actually visit. As a child, my dream city was Greenville, Mississippi, twenty-eight miles north of where we lived. Philadelphia, Pennsylvania, spoke of a way of living I could not even imagine.

But I never forgot those conversations held around an open fire at Cousin Lula's back in Glen Allan. From her we heard about black people who had lived free in Philadelphia while slavery was the law throughout the South. Philadelphia was a magical place to me, and it became even more so as my schooling introduced me to the founding fathers and the crafting of our Constitution and Bill of Rights. Though born in challenging circumstances as an African American in the South, I grew up with a thirst to know our nation's history. So to be in Philadelphia, where so much of our nation's formation had taken place, was to make real my childhood imagination.

I found it ironic that my 2000 conversation in Philadelphia would not be about the founding fathers, but about the ordinary people—Cousin Lula Harris and Mama Ponk and so many others—who were part of my small "colored" community and who made the value of community real through their daily living. On the morning of my speech, the capacity audience that filled the Wyndham Hotel ballroom allowed me to transport them to the Mississippi Delta and, like Cousin Lula Harris did for me, I told them the endearing stories about our simple life, and how my folks transformed living on my behalf.

The audience leaned into my conversation about these ordinary work-ing people who, despite the rigors of legal segregation, had demonstrated through their selflessness the power and the impact of building community. This was the key point of my talk. I was not there to rail against the racism I grew up with. I was there to tell the story and show some old photographs of a small community of ordinary people who had battled racism and legal segregation by unselfishly building a community for me. Over the years, I had distilled their courageous and selfless behavior into eight timeless and universal lessons, the subject of *The Eight Habits of the Heart.* I offered these timeless habits as universal principles to my international audience that morning.

It was an audience of educators, people whose profession holds the key to the future for our world. I wanted them to know that those eight principles can be accessed to build community despite challenging circumstances. I had seen and experienced this strong community of ordinary people I loved. I wanted my audience to know that the habits are not mere concepts but can be and must be embodied by real people, like my "colored" elders, like us.

That morning, with my keynote address over, and after shaking a few hands and making promises to stay in touch, I made my way from the hotel's lower level to the upper lobby, now crowded with rushing guests. Apparently, the hotel was hosting several conferences at the same time. The escalators, elevators, and main lobby were jammed with people, all wearing badges and talking loudly, yelling for others to wait and for the bell captain to hail them a cab.

As I walked through this bedlam, I could hardly wait to get to the quiet of my room. Then I was suddenly—along with everybody else in the crowded lobby—startled by a distinctive Southern female voice. The voice rose high above all the chatter. It was obvious that some white lady was impatiently trying to get somebody's attention.

I hurried on toward the bank of elevators. But as I tried to push through the crowd, I could still hear that distinct Southern voice calling out for someone to wait up. It was becoming a bit irritating. *I wish that lady would find whoever she's looking for,* I thought to myself, with no idea yet that this female voice was saying, "Mister Taulbert, Mister Taulbert, wait up, please." I guess "Taulbert" was lost in the crowd noise and obscured by her Southern enunciation. I don't remember if I slowed down, hit a traffic jam, or the female with the Southern voice started to run. All I know is that before I reached the elevators, I realized that she was, indeed, calling my name. Looking in her direction, I recognized that the owner of the voice was rushing through the crowded lobby toward me with several other white ladies in tow.

"Mister Taulbert, Mister Taulbert, please wait up, will you wait up, please?"

I stopped in my tracks. The lady, backed by her group, now had my attention, but she continued calling out my name and waving her conference program. When the group finally reached me, she immediately started talking, speaking to me face-to-face and eye-to-eye, as if she had known me for years.

"Now, Mister Taulbert, you just did a splendid job this morning." Her companions were all nodding and trying to speak as well, but the lady out front, obviously the spokesperson, continued: "Mister Taulbert, you did a great job. You really brought the concept of community home to all of us. We just loved your stories and the vintage pictures. Didn't you, ladies?"

"Yes, those pictures took us all back to a place we recalled from our childhood as well," another lady said to a chorus of nods and verbal agreement. Our not having been introduced didn't matter to these women. The lead lady began retelling me my own speech, recalling names and places as if my story had been hers. I was taken aback. I stood and listened as this white lady, with a gratitude that seemed entirely genuine, thanked me for introducing her and her friends to my Mississippi Delta "porch people," the ordinary "colored" folks from my small town, like Cousin Lula Harris and Mama Ponk, who built a sense of community in spite of the challenges of a legally segregated world.

That constricted world had for the most part been created by white folks who looked like these ladies who had just chased me across the hotel lobby. Somehow the stories from my community had resonated with them, just as Cousin Lula's stories about Philadelphia had resonated with me so many years earlier. I could see the impact on these white women's faces, but I was still somewhat surprised at the attention they had paid to stories primarily about Southern African Americans. They had heard me talk about the daily personal slights our people faced and how such hurtful bigotry had been dealt with to ensure that I would have a good future despite it all. I was talking about the world that had existed, no doubt right across the street from themselves, so to speak, and at a time when that world—our "colored" world—could just as well have been on the other side of the ocean. Though we were standing together and talking about a shared place and time, I knew that, historically, we had come from separate worlds. Listening to these white ladies' accents straight out of the Deep South, I was suddenly transported back into the days when such a conversation would not have been held.

I listened intently, though, and in amazement to Southern white strangers recalling with great clarity much of what I had said that morning about how my community had been built and how its people had lived by timeless and universal principles. After a few moments, only the most vocal lady was still talking, but she had breath to spare for all of them.

"Mister Taulbert," she said, "I am Camille Nairn. We're all from South Carolina, near Columbia. Obviously, your talk meant much to us. We are Southerners, too, you know. Except for Dr. Paget here, we all work with the South Carolina State Department of Education. Dr. Paget is our program evaluator. She works with the university."

Camille Nairn seemed determined to call me "Mister Taulbert" at nearly every turn. "Now, Mister Taulbert, we want you to come to South Carolina.

This is just the message our people need to hear. We all agree. Now, who do we have to contact? Your agent or whoever represents you? I know you are no doubt booked up, but you've got to find some time for us."

This lady was as convincing as anyone could be that I needed to come to South Carolina. Though I could tell that she was not going to take "no" for an answer, I must admit that going to South Carolina was not a priority on my agenda. Hers was one of those Southern states, like my home state of Mississippi, that seemed to have had great difficulty in moving beyond the past. Her invitation ushered in multiple feelings, cautiousness, and, for me as a national speaker, expectations as well. Initially, the cautiousness took front seat. I hesitated to give her an immediate answer. Maybe it was because of that clear Southern diction—sounds from my childhood, from the other side of town, sounds that did not carry the best of memories. So much was crowding into my head and heart—all associated with my being black and with their being white and Southern.

Obviously, much had changed socially between the races in the South. Yet I remembered the divided world I grew up in. *Little Cliff lived there still.* Besides, how could I be sure her South Carolina audience would welcome my stories of my black family with gracious acceptance? Could whites possibly share the same pride with which I would tell my people's stories? I had only their stories to tell, but how could white Southerners possibly welcome my speech and me?

The invitation sounded gracious and sincere. Outwardly, I listened politely, but inwardly, I had my doubts. This was not an invitation to come back to Philadelphia where Negroes had lived free in an era of slavery, nor an invitation to Bangor, Maine, where the Underground Railroad made a difference in so many lives. It was an invitation to South Carolina—a state that represented a past I wanted to forget and a modern history that was still troubling. Senator Strom Thurmond had not gone out of his way to leave me with a reason to savor such a visit. This was his state. His stance on race was clearly articulated. South Carolina had been the first state to secede, starting the Civil War to defend the institution of slavery, and it continued to revere the Southern rebellion, so there was not much room for me to be overcome with excitement.

The sounds of Philadelphia all around me—horns honking, tires squealing, people laughing and talking—were no match for the conversation in my head. While those filling the hotel lobby around me were preparing to see the Liberty Bell and other historical monuments, my head was elsewhere, trying to understand whether this lady could be right and my presence in South Carolina might make a difference.

But I kept quiet and politely listened. Mrs. Nairn, obviously not having the same conversation in her head, just kept talking to me as if the Civil War had never happened and the civil rights movement was a bygone conclusion.

"Mister Taulbert, just ever'body in the county is coming to this conference," she said in that certain Southern tone. "You'd be the perfect speaker for us." And then she just stood there, waiting. She was determined to have an answer right then, right there in the hotel lobby.

I wanted to ask if the audience would be racially mixed. Where would this event be held? Would black people be invited? Would it be held in a place that was historically for whites only? Everything emanating from Mrs. Nairn's voice spoke of a different South Carolina, not the one that lingered in my head. I wanted to ask those questions, but couldn't bring myself to do it. Finally, bracing myself and pushing beyond the talk in my head, I agreed that if my schedule permitted, I would come to South Carolina. The ladies all gave sighs of relief. We shook hands, exchanged cards, and went our separate ways.

WITHIN MONTHS, I FOUND myself in Columbia, South Carolina. It was just as Camille Nairn said it would be. Everyone from around the county was there, or so it seemed. Contrary to all that went through my head in

that hotel lobby in Philadelphia, I was at ease giving my talk about growing up "colored" in the South and all that entailed, even as I dramatically
pointed out how powerful and protective my community had been for a
little boy who looked like me. Somehow these South Carolinians rallied to
my people's unselfishness as a characteristic still needed today—not just to
fight racism, but as the antidote to *any* negative virus that would seek to
destroy our children.

As I had done in Philadelphia, I took my listeners to Glen Allan, my
hometown, and to the people who personified community for me. I piled
them inside my great-grandfather's 1949 Buick and took them to Greenville,
Mississippi, where holding my grandfather's hand was required so that I
would not give in to youthful curiosity and find myself in places identified
as "White Only." I took them to church, where my elders refueled their
lives for another week of demanding labor. I invited them to supper, where
"saying grace" was required and where the grease and butter were stirred to
perfection. I gave them an insight into the community that had protected
and nurtured my life. The audience applauded loudly when I finished my
talk—a talk about African American survival, though not labeled as such. I
could see Camille Nairn in the audience and could tell that she was pleased.

Needless to say, and as expected by my host, I also talked about the
"eight habits of the heart" and their transformative effect when unselfishly
embraced and applied. I offered my life as the proof. As I had expected,
Civil War statues were everywhere in Columbia, but they didn't have the
emotional impact upon me I had dreaded. I wanted to believe that this
Southern city was growing up. It looked that way. Although my audience
was primarily a Southern white audience—and all those white people applauded loudly—the conference attendees included educators and local
religious and political leaders, and black people were among them. I was
delighted to see that.

Camille—I had observed by now that everyone called her that—cornered me when the speech was over. "Mister Taulbert, I told you so. I just knew that your stories were ours. They were just what we needed to hear. You think it went all right, don't you?"

"Yes, I think it did," I replied, as I made ready to autograph my books. We saw the long line of people waiting and smiled at each other with satisfaction. As I settled myself at the autographing table, I told her, "I guess you were right. We are Southern and in spite of everything, our lives are really intertwined." That small moment in time called for music—the music I remembered from back home, "Trouble Don't Last Always," a rousing and jubilant song of triumph—if only for a short while.

"I told you so," she replied as she walked away and left me signing books.

2

Watching and Remembering

"In childhood, we press our nose to the pane, looking out. In
memories of childhood, we press our nose to the pane, looking in."
—*Robert Brault*

As I ENDED MY DAY IN COLUMBIA, I WAS PLEASANTLY SURPRISED
that everything had turned out so well. Though surrounded by Southerners, many of whom did not look like me and who spoke in the accents of
white power I remembered from my childhood, I maintained my outward
composure. Inwardly, I felt apprehensive. My reality and my head were
somewhat at odds. Even as I shook appreciative hands, my head remained
on the alert for the backlash I fully expected would come at any moment.
There had been too many lessons of race and place in my childhood, telling
me not to assume anything.

All in all, though, I had to admit it was a good day. I somehow credited
its success to being in Columbia, an urban city seemingly committed to
carving a new future from its contentious past. With the speech behind me,
and Camille and her friends pleased, the voices in my head quieted. I turned
to the next leg of my journey. I headed back home to Tulsa, Oklahoma,
to prepare myself for work in Europe where I would conduct community
building workshops for the K-12 leadership of our Department of Defense
schools throughout Germany.

Somewhere between Tulsa and Germany, however, I was again stopped by that same voice that had hailed me in Philadelphia's Wyndham Hotel lobby. Camille Nairn was calling my name again, but this time on the phone. I was invited to be a guest in Allendale County, Camille's hometown. Her invitation to Allendale was just as effusive as the invitation to Columbia had been. From Camille's invitation, one could expect Allendale to be a college town and not far from Hilton Head Island, which had its own persona. I had done Columbia, so why not Allendale? Those challenging racial moments I had feared had not occurred, and besides, the food was just to my liking—all the secret ingredients of Southern cooking.

I accepted the invitation.

WITHIN MONTHS I WAS back in South Carolina. Exiting the airplane, I could hardly wait to stretch my legs and be on my way to Allendale. As I walked through the Columbia Airport with its strategically placed white rocking chairs, I reflexively kept my guard up. I knew Camille would meet me, and, if all was the same, she would not graciously extend her hand as one professional to the other but would give me a hug right in front of every white Southerner and every black person watching. I really wanted the handshake, so easy to explain and somewhat acceptable. While I was pulling my luggage, I spotted Camille and I also spotted her smile. She was not going to shake my hand. I could feel it, even though we were far from each other across the airport lobby. As we got closer, I braced myself; it was a train I couldn't stop.

"Mister Taulbert, it's so good to have you back here with us," she gushed as she gave me the foreseen hug. I made sure that I didn't meet the eye of a single person—black or white—who might have been trying to figure out this reunion. With my luggage in tow and our conversation in high gear, we walked to her car, where she introduced me to her husband. *Why didn't he come in with her? I could have hugged them both.*

"Mister Taulbert, I want you to meet my husband, Alan. Now, Alan is not a Southerner like us. He's from across the waters." Alan, somewhat short and appearing very intellectual, was quick to reach out his hand and welcome me with his eyes. I attributed this to the fact that he was from "across the waters"—another Mason-Dixon Line of sorts. Like Philadelphia, Europe was a magical place where color was not the sole determining factor.

"Alan, it's my pleasure. Say, where are you from? Since you're not a true-blooded Southerner like me and Camille."

"I am a transplant, Clifton, here at the university. I'm from a place called Newcastle upon Tyne in England. I love Europe, but I must say that there are things about your South that I really enjoy." Alan turned out to be a well-known geologist and disseminator of new geological ideas and concepts around the world. But as I learned, he was slowly becoming a Southerner, especially in the ways of food.

His British accent and immediate engagement left little room for the expected voices in my head to sound their cautionary alarm. He was unlike the picture that my childhood voices had anticipated for the husband of a South Carolina white woman like Camille, an older white male for whom there was no need to shake hands or hold pleasant conversations with folks like me. One never forgets how to be "colored," and I still know how to respond in those severely defined situations. But Alan, with all the physical characteristics of his Southern counterparts, left me with no uncomfortable feelings. His genuine handshake startled the voices of caution, and for a while they kept quiet.

CAMILLE DROVE US QUICKLY through the airport exit. Now that we were settled in and headed to our destination, I embraced the back seat as a place to rest and unwind. In the confines of their car, I felt no need to validate my presence with accolades from others about my personal accomplishments—accomplishments that Little Cliff's circumstances should have made nearly impossible. I simply felt welcomed.

We drove from the airport and through the city. For a while the South that haunted me stayed outside the car. As we left Columbia in the rearview mirror, I kept connecting my destination to some beautiful place with much to see and do. I could hardly wait—that is, until Camille chimed in with her very vivid description of Allandale.

"Clifton, Allendale is not like Columbia, or Hilton Head, for that matter. My small community is much like your Mississippi hometown. You know, I recognized so much of Allendale when I first heard you talk. Like Glen Allan, Allendale is as flat as a pancake and equally as hot. And the humidity surrounds us like cheap steam. But we're used to it down here, ain't we, Alan?"

"Not really," Alan answered.

I smiled, but Camille's description startled me. I had created a totally different mental picture. As much as I enjoyed going home, I was prepared right then to be someplace else. It wasn't her description of the heat that bothered me, but her reference to our hometowns being so similar. The heat and humidity I could handle, but now I was unsure of how I would be received. Little Cliff clearly understood the domination of race and place in small towns and rural counties across the South. The former slave states, the states of the Confederacy, have always been socially and culturally connected.

But before I could say anything, Alan continued. "I still haven't gotten used to this insufferable heat. Thank God, they do have air conditioning down here."

"Now, Clifton," my hostess said, "don't let Alan scare you off. The heat's good for the cotton, the peach trees and the corn—well, just about ever'thing we grow down here." Camille made sure to keep the view of the South in the proper perspective, and without reference to the history that hung above both our heads.

However, as we bantered back and forth, and with the skyline of Columbia no longer in sight, the poor, rural South I knew so well began to show up outside the car windows—bringing with it personal memories of certain aspects of that life I had worked so hard to leave behind. I was in South Carolina, but the landscape we were passing through might as well have been Glen Allan or my wife's hometown of Eudora, Arkansas.

I recognized all that I was seeing and could imagine all that I couldn't see. Maybe this ride through the countryside was commonplace for Camille and Alan, but for me it was taking on a different meaning. I was seeing my own life every time we passed a small, wood-framed home with black kids running and playing together in the bare yards.

It didn't matter that Camille had met me in Philadelphia and that Alan was from England. In the back seat of their car, I was seeing myself as the little "colored" boy from back home.

I knew that part of my talk in Allendale would have to do with what their county and community could do together to overcome the challenges of poverty that still handicapped their schools. Commenting on all that I was observing as we rode along would have been a great start to that conversation. Instead, Camille and Alan were quiet in the front seat, and, except for my interior conversation, so was I. It had become very easy for me to talk onstage in front of hundreds or even thousands about the poverty I'd faced as a young boy; it was not so easy when riding with white friends.

As I kept silent, I wondered if the Southern landscape of poverty moved Camille and Alan as it was moving me. It didn't need a graph or statistics to grab my heart. Looking out the car windows, I was seeing real kids, living in a real world, where our flawed past continued to impact their future.

That view from the back seat was all too familiar to me. I recognized Glen Allan, my home community. Poverty has a look of sameness and is easily recognizable wherever it manifests. I hated the small, cramped shotgun homes that had once housed many of my kin. I no longer lived in such a house, but I was seeing them as we drove. They still dotted the South Carolina landscape, not as a historical reminder, but as homes, just as they had existed when I was growing up. They looked the same, each with a front door off the porch that gave you a view straight through the house. I had been in so many of them. I had spent many nights crowded in a double bed with cousins or friends. I had sat around many a makeshift dining table with families who had only the food from the land.

Emerging out of nowhere were kids, just like my cousins and me, rolling abandoned tires. I could see their faces and imagine their laughter. They were creative, just as we had been, making do with what the world offered. This was the world to which they were introduced and which was just as I remembered—yards where no flowers or grass grew, just dirt and dust everywhere. It was the twenty-first century and they were playing the same games I had played in the mid-twentieth. I was in South Carolina, but with all that I was seeing, Camille was right, I felt as if I was indeed headed home to the childhood world I had left behind.

I was overwrought by what I was seeing—the way of life of "colored" people that hadn't changed. The impact of our Southern way of life had a long reach—one that was still seen and felt. Here were black children as poor as we were before the civil rights legislation and anti-poverty programs of the 1960s that were supposed to change all this.

I wondered if Camille and Alan were feeling the same. But then, how could they? They had not lived my life from the inside. Legal segregation had not been their lot, nor, from what I could tell, had they ever been poor. As I grappled with my history, they were quietly listening to soothing music and keeping cool in the circulating air.

Even though I recognized all that I was seeing, I didn't want what I was seeing to be a norm that would never change. I had escaped rearing my own children in a shotgun house, and I wanted the same for the kids outside the car window. I wondered if those kids had any idea that a really big world existed beyond their front porches. Had they ever traveled to Columbia, their state capital, or had the opportunity to visit Hilton Head Island? I was sure I knew the answers. I only had to remember my own confinement to a small geographical location. For me to just get to Greenville, Mississippi, our county seat, was tantamount to taking the Concorde to Paris, in the words of Paul Galloway, one of my reviewers, a celebrated columnist for the *Chicago Tribune*. And Greenville was only twenty-six miles from Glen Allan.

My great-grandpa had been instrumental in changing my scenery. Our very infrequent trips to Greenville kept my mind from becoming locked in, from accepting what I saw daily to be what I would see forever. As a young boy, I had never heard of the North Sea. But decades later I was there. I can still see myself standing on a Scottish bluff overlooking that great body of water.

I knew that the impossible could become possible for these kids. I myself could have easily been left alongside the road, if not for the unselfishness of others who crafted a vision for me that I may not have understood at the time, but that left me with the idea that I could do more. This is what I wanted for those kids. I knew that good community was essential to accomplishing this feat. Had I not experienced such a process, I probably never would have discovered the writer who lived inside me. Writing had become the ticket that introduced me to the world beyond the Mississippi Delta, to audiences in England, Japan, Germany, and Scotland, and was now taking me to a community called Allendale.

With the music playing on the car stereo, I leaned back and thought deeply about my childhood church back in the Mississippi Delta. I thought of Daddy Julius Chaney, the senior deacon, and how he would be humming as he made his way up front to start the church services, and we would all be humming with him. For a few minutes, no real words were needed, just our connected humming as we lifted ourselves above the labor that defined our lives. Our humming was just as critical to the process of building community as the acts of unselfishness that I experienced. I wanted to hum now, but instead I closed my eyes and remembered how the transformative process of community building had changed my life.

Camille was right. Looking out the car windows had shown me anew that my journey was bigger than my personal story. Others needed to hear about the power of their unselfish and caring presence in the lives of others.

I had chronicled this process in my first book, *Once Upon a Time When We Were Colored*. Speaking to the Allendale community would give me that opportunity again. Now that I knew it would not take place in an urban setting, I just hoped that my audience would be receptive to my conversation. Camille said they would be. I had to wait and see. I know that the impossible is possible. This is my conversation. Somehow I had to stir up within my audience an understanding of the importance of educating every child equally and giving each a vision for a future that included them.

I WAS SO ENGAGED in my own thoughts that I hadn't noticed that we had pulled off the main road onto a small side street. My head was still in Scotland, I suppose, and I had every one of those kids with me, looking in awe at the world that surrounded us.

"Are we there?" I asked.

"Not yet. We're just stopping by the house to let Alan off. He has some work to do with his plants. I swear, he's always planting something." Camille was talking to me through the rearview mirror. Alan was quiet as we pulled up to their home with its well-manicured yard—no used tires to roll—so different from the shotgun houses I had seen earlier.

I shook hands with Alan and we promised to stay in touch. As he made his way into the house, I moved to the front seat. Camille and I chit-chatted as she drove—she was not afraid to put her foot to the pedal—but nothing was said about the countryside we had just passed through or the life we had both observed through the windows as we drove by. We talked about the afternoon and who would be there. Camille said again that my talk was what they really needed to hear. I don't know how long we drove before

Camille pulled off the two-lane country road onto the well-paved entry to the Salkehatchie campus of the University of South Carolina, where I would speak.

"Folks are already here to hear you," Camille observed as we traded the comfort of the air-conditioned car for the outside heat and a swarm of really big Southern mosquitoes. The stifling humidity was overbearing and very much like in Mississippi.

I might as well be picking cotton back home with all this heat. I'll be so sweaty by the time we get inside that no one will want to get close to me.

I was feeling a deep sense of familiarity as I looked around, seeing flatness that never ended.

I know this place. I know this smell. I know I haven't been here, but I know this place. Camille was right. No wonder my talk about Glen Allan reminded her of her hometown.

My head was buzzing with conversation. As quickly as I could, I made my way out of the heat and into the college auditorium. I took a deep breath and inhaled the welcome air-conditioned coolness. Then I scanned the audience for people who looked like me. Given the demographics of the area, I was expecting to see a large number of African Americans. Instead, I saw white faces all over the room. I felt disappointment, but also understanding. Though much change had taken place, social gatherings were still challenges to overcome. I finally spotted a group of faces that looked like mine. I gave a great sigh of relief.

The four well-dressed black people were sitting together, their paper plates in their laps and their cups of sweet tea on the floor beside their chairs. Their presence verified that the times had changed, but if they were at all like me, they were also somewhat cautious, clearly remembering the way it was. I did not hesitate to go over and shake their hands and thank them for coming out. "I am Clifton Taulbert, one of your speakers today. Thank you for being here."

"We saw the flyer," the older man said as we shook hands. "So, you are not from around here?"

Before I could reply, one of the ladies spoke up. "Of course not, they brought him in." Turning to me, she said, "But we need people like you to open our eyes and ears."

"Well, I am going to talk about the community of people who raised me while I was growing up on the Mississippi Delta."

The same lady spoke up again. "You know, I got folks in Mississippi."

"I think every black person in South Carolina has people in Mississippi. Some of my folks came from here as well—that is, the early ones—those who were slaves. Do you know your Mississippi relatives?" I asked.

"No, sir, we lost contact after the older folks died and all."

"I understand. I don't know my South Carolina relatives, either, but I am so glad you all are here."

They were gracious.

Has the South really changed? I thought to myself as I walked away. To go home with them would provide the assessment of change that challenged my thinking. Back within the safety of their homes, they would discuss all that had taken place and what was real and what was phony. I could not help but laugh. I felt like I was in Glen Allan, and I could hear B. B. King telling us once again the thrill was gone, telling us once again that actions speak louder than words. I chuckled to myself.

As I made my way through the crowd, I could hear voices around me. It was an all too familiar sound. Much of the talk and the laughter reminded me of the white "straw bosses" and my days in the fields when I was picking and chopping cotton. The sound was powerful. I hate to admit it, but the sound took me back, maybe too far back, almost to total ignorance of the fact of who I was now and the reason for my presence. I could feel that attitude of "them and us" trying to creep into my consciousness.

As my past and present collided, I began to lose a bit of the "citizen of the world" confidence I usually had, or at least tried to portray. I began to wonder if the speech I delivered in Philadelphia, and even that in Columbia, would resonate with this completely rural Southern crowd. Would they really want to hear about a powerful and caring community built by black folks despite how badly they had been mistreated? My talk would center on the black fieldworkers and maids—my people—not the life of plantation owners, as I felt sure some of these white people had to be.

3

The Chasm That Separated Our World

"When you grow up in a totally segregated society, where everybody around you believes that segregation is proper, you have a hard time. You can't believe how much it's a part of your thinking."
—Shelby Foote

WHILE THE MAJORITY OF THE ALLENDALE CROWD MINGLED as old friends, I should have been employing my creativity on the speech I would give, or better still, shaking hands and making connections for the future. Instead, my thoughts were divided by the pressure of feeling slightly out of place while at the same time knowing I was in the right place. Who better to talk about the power of community than someone who had been a beneficiary of the community building process?

I was determined to tuck my insecurities behind the gray suit, white shirt, and appropriately striped tie. I refused to let these South Carolinians see me sweat. I knew how to do this, to push down out of my consciousness familiar internal conversations that were the lessons of race and place, once the protocol of our daily living. Today, in the twenty-first century, I was determined to be the scholar and not to be intimidated by white faces that in times past had cast me as someone insignificant.

Finally, the program started. I quietly listened, smiled appropriately, and waved when necessary. When the time came for me to be introduced,

I sat up, squared my shoulders, and focused on the four black people in the audience.

The introduction by Camille could not have been better.

"I'm so glad you all came today. We have an excellent speaker. I heard him in Philadelphia, and we brought him to Columbia some months ago. He did such an outstanding job we just had to have him here with us today in Allendale."

I was looking out at the crowd as she talked. I wanted to make sure that they were taking it all in. They were listening, all of them, to her characterization of my talk and how our paths had crossed. So I waited for Camille to complete her introduction.

"He's a Southerner just like us. Don't let his resumé fool you. He's traveled the world—from China to Central America—but he was born right down the road so to speak . . . in little Glen Allan, Mississippi." She went on to recount the Philadelphia story and welcomed me as one of them. Then it was my time to speak.

After receiving a quick, validating hug from Camille, I waited while the applause quieted. I felt as if all eyes were upon me, and voices out of the past were loud in my head. Were they ill at ease as they waited to hear what I would say? Would I bring up subjects that should best be left alone? Would I make them feel guilty for the past of their fathers and mothers, a past not far removed from all of us? They were all watching me. I could feel their eyes.

And of course, I felt the eyes of the four black people, because I was watching them. The one lady had told me that Allendale needed to hear me, but would I say something that would make their lives difficult after I had boarded the plane for home? I was being challenged by the past and dared by the future. As conflicted as I felt, I had to rise to the occasion.

I had been just as intimidated a decade earlier in Las Vegas, when I made one of my first public addresses to about three thousand white people at the American Booksellers Association's annual conference in 1990. I shared the stage with Donald Trump and Isabelle Allende. I had no tall buildings to talk about and no relatives who would have been the president of a country. I had to be me. And when I stood up to speak, as nervous as I was, being from the Delta was the story I told.

In Allendale, this would be my challenge again, to take a mainly white and this time Southern audience down dusty roads of the Delta and into the small shotgun homes most people saw only through their car windows. I refused to allow the voices of caution in my head to paralyze me. I took a deep breath and quickly dove into the speech. My theme was the power of community to bring about the sustained change they were seeking for their county, from education to health reform to economic growth. And of course I used the example of my "porch people" to emphasize the power of ordinary people to bring about such change. "Porch people" is the collective name I had given to all the caring elders who had surrounded my life growing up. I wanted my speech to galvanize Allendale's thinking on what was possible if they were brave enough to reach beyond the past and embrace the future together.

As I talked about my great-grandfather, Poppa Joe Young, and his 1949 Buick, as well as his efforts to show me love and care no matter how the outside world treated him, I could see heads nodding as if they understood exactly what I was saying. These were my stories, but some of those nodding were white and they were on the path with me. I could also see the four black guests nodding approval as their eyes told me that they had experienced similar unselfishness while they were growing up. With their nods and the nods of those who seemed to have clearly understood, I drove on, piling all who wanted to go with me in the front seat of Poppa's car.

I had learned that I could share my space and still get to my personal destination. Helping people to understand this lesson is central to my lectures. Other people matter. Our individual, personal journey is not necessarily the most important agenda on the planet.

For a brief time that afternoon, we were all together in my Mississippi Delta. For many, this was their first time inside the homes and lives of the "colored" people they had only seen at a safe distance or as employees, where no substantive conversations were ever held.

Camille was right again. This conversation about community seemed to have been hitting the target.

And so I talked and told my story. At the conclusion of my speech, I was met with a standing ovation, and then there were closing words from a black man from Columbia who had come in after I arrived. When the program was over, I moved with all the rest of the guests to a reception that followed.

As I made my move to join the four black guests, I could hear the voice of Little Cliff pointing out a reality that he knew all too well.

When this is over, I bet they will go their separate ways as always—back to a world of their own and the whites back to theirs.

Little Cliff was not too far wrong. As loud as the applause had been, the speech was over, and they were back to their reality, one where being divided by race and maybe even station in life is acceptable. That's just how it looked to me as the circles formed for the reception. I wasn't mad. I knew where I was. I was just hurt that it took less than five minutes for them to resegregate themselves.

Right then I wanted to yell, "Stop!" I wanted to deliver my speech about community all over again, louder and hopefully clearer. I wanted them all to understand where community really starts. A discussion of possibilities doesn't get us very far. Community needed to start right here and right now, with the people within our reach.

When I left the South in 1963, I thought I would be rid of all of that racial separation—those ever-present lessons, admonitions, and warnings—once I crossed the Mason-Dixon Line. I was seventeen and a high school graduate when I went north to St. Louis. Here, I falsely assumed, the lessons that kept me safe in the South would not be needed; the color of skin would never again be an issue, and I would never have to listen to the voices of caution. Lessons that had been so necessary to keep a young black boy safe in the Jim Crow South also brought with them intimidation and a devalued sense of self. Whereas the nation and the world validated the superiority of being white, I had to be intentional about valuing myself, as did the community that surrounded me.

As I continued to make my way through the Allendale crowd that afternoon, I realized that our shared generation had missed many opportunities to remodel our world as we passed through it. As Southern baby boomers, most of us had not been raised to embrace a shared kinship, one that stretched across racial, social and economic lines. Incredible opportunities to build an inclusive community have been missed along the way. As former Supreme Court Justice Sandra Day O'Connor said, "Nothing of worth is accomplished alone." Community teaches us to become weavers, and to welcome the variety of threads into our lives. That was the essence of my speech, and now I wanted them to understand that the call for action was not for tomorrow or for someone else. It was for all of us, right here and now.

Protocol finally took over, and with the rims of glasses being tapped to get everyone's attention, my mind was brought back to the program. A reception line was formed for the speakers, and with Camille by my side, I found myself embracing the opportunity—sharing bits of conversation with some as the line moved and people passed from one speaker to the next. I could shake hands and hold polite conversation as Camille introduced me to all the people she knew, especially the guests she had invited. In such a setting, there should have been no feelings of intimidation, but even as I shook hands and smiled, I still knew I was black and in the South. I had been invited, but history had not provided me a chair at this table. That's just the way it was, and I stood and smiled as Camille continued her magic.

"Mister Taulbert, you let me know if I can get you something. Now, I want you to make sure you meet the man who spoke after you. He's from

Columbia. He's with the NAACP, you know. You'll enjoy knowing him. Do you need to take a bathroom break? If so, just let me know and we can take care of that."

Camille Nairn, I must say, was unusual and went out of her way to create an environment that made me feel welcome. Although we never had a conversation about it, I felt that she was well aware of where we were and what that could mean for me. Laws had been enacted to move us toward equality, but the timetable for change was within our personal power. And for some, the time had not yet come. Camille never once asked what I was thinking in quiet moments when I should have been carried away in conversation. She sensed something, because every so often she would ask if I was comfortable or if everything was all right. She knew that her Southern world had not been designed to make me feel welcomed and comfortable in such a social setting.

"Mister Taulbert—you all right?"

"Camille, I'm fine. It's just that I don't know any of these people."

"That's all right, Sugar. They know you."

I was in South Carolina's Low Country, and she was well aware of the racial history that surrounded us. Without any doubt, her assuring words meant much to me and allowed me to continue smiling while shaking hands with people I didn't know and whose presence that day evoked memories I wished to have forgotten.

4

Standing Alone,
Surrounded by History

"Each player must accept the cards life deals him or her: but once they are in hand, he or she alone must decide how to play the cards in order to win the game." —Voltaire

IT WOULD HAVE BEEN COMFORTING TO SLIP OFF TO THE SIDE and deflect the memories that were crowding into my head, but I couldn't do that. People were still in line and I was still shaking hands, with Camille beside me as we greeted people and she thanked them for coming.

Between greetings, she turned to me and said enthusiastically, "Mister Taulbert, I told you in Philadelphia that you'd fit right in. You are a Southerner just like us." I just smiled. Sometimes a smile is the best conversation, and this was one of those times.

Camille got a signal from someone in the back of the hall and said, "Now you just wait right here. I'll be back. Want me to bring some sweet tea?"

"No, I'll be fine. I'll just wait till you get back."

While she was gone, I looked around and didn't see the four black people. I guess they had called it a day. Their quick getaway reminded me of myself; I can remember how, being at the right place but feeling out of place, a quick getaway served me well. I did see the black guy from Columbia who was with the NAACP. He seemed to know several of the white guests. I watched as he went through the crowd, shaking hands. I was not about to move. I had my orders from Camille, and I was staying in place.

I was still finding it amusing, strange, and fulfilling that the reason for my invitation here had been my hometown of Glen Allan—the source of all of Little Cliff's remembered lessons that were making me uncomfortable this day.

But then my reflection was interrupted by a flurry of activity beyond the reception line near the back of the hall. It was getting everybody's attention, and I stopped shaking hands to see what was going on.

Those of us in the receiving line had lost the spotlight, and my eyes followed the sounds to where a small crowd was gathering. The conversation in my head ramped up.

Where is Camille? Sure is a lot of buzz. I wonder what's going on back there. Must be the Mayor or someone like that. Camille knows everybody.

Finally, over the commotion, I heard her distinctive Southern voice rising, just as it had that morning in Philadelphia several years earlier. Then I saw her emerging from the small crowd and heading back towards me. I breathed a sigh of relief, but I also noticed that with her was an older white lady, very petite and well-dressed. Most of the women were dressed for comfort on this hot day, but not this lady. She was all dressed up for an "occasion." She really stood out. I could not imagine who she might be.

I stood in my spot and waited as guests jockeyed for position to shake the older lady's hand. I saw the NAACP speaker hug the little white lady and they talked, seemingly with great familiarity.

They sure seem to know each other. I guess some things have changed. They almost ran into each other's arms. I know she's white . . . or really light black.

I couldn't really make out her face because she kept turning to hug or pat someone on the hand. I noticed, though, that Camille never left her side. *She must be really important!* With all that had gone on in my head that afternoon, I continued to watch as she and the black man talked, leaning in toward each other as if no one was there but them. She finally moved on. I kept watching. It wasn't a long distance, but it was taking Camille and this older lady forever to get to the front of the auditorium. From all the attention, I knew she had to be important—someone Camille wanted to make sure that I met.

Camille continued to pull her guest in my direction, trying to wave off some who wanted a word with her. As they got closer, I could see urgency written all over Camille's face, but not on the face of the lady walking beside her. In spite of Camille almost pulling her toward me, the lady continued to shake another hand or pat another head or give a kiss on another cheek. I could hardly wait to meet this person whom everyone seemed to know.

Finally, we were face to face. An odd silence briefly defined the moment, and I could feel an uneasiness settling over me, which in itself made little sense seeing that Camille had a broad, contented smile on her face. My eyes focused on the small lady who accompanied her and somehow seemed bigger than her physical stature. The silence ended when Camille gushed out an introduction, as only she could do.

"Mister Taulbert, I want you to meet Mama."

Her mother, I thought to myself, *surely not.*

"Your mother?"

"Most surely, Mister Taulbert. This is my mother, Mrs. Camille Cunningham Sharp."

Maybe it had to do with the way she was dressed or how people had responded to her and she to them. All I know is that while standing in front of her, and as small as she was, that uneasiness I had felt earlier began to morph into recognizable feelings of intimidation. Instead of focusing on my present surroundings, memories flooded in from Glen Allan of older white women to whom we paid respect. I was tongue-tied for a brief moment. I had not expected the lady whom the crowd had so eagerly welcomed to be my host's mother. Nor had I expected her presence to evoke such memories.

Even though I had seen her hug the black guy from Columbia, at the moment that memory was not providing me any ease. All the while—only seconds, really—she kept her composure, standing quietly with her eyes directly on me. Maybe that was the reason for the feelings that were surging inside my head; her eyes were not averted, but directly on mine. Our eyes were locked. I knew I had to say something. I had just been introduced. Fortunately for me and maybe for the both of us, her daughter broke through the impasse to rescue the moment.

"Yes, Mister Taulbert, this is Mama. Yes, we both have the same name." Camille was quick to point this out, obviously having done this before, as she beamed from ear to ear. Her mother was still quiet, her eyes directly on me, but a smile was forming. In spite of Camille's excitement and the smile on her mother's face, I remained uneasy. Then, before I had to force myself to say anything, her mother extended her hand, which to that point had been gracefully folded across the purse she held in front of her.

In that moment, I didn't feel the natural response to immediately reach out. My head was holding me back. Little Cliff was frightened to make such a move. Then I pushed through the voices in my head and extended my adult hand, even though on the inside I was that black child in Glen Allan. Familiar and comforting music, the strains of Muddy Waters, was filtering into my head, soulful and defiant. That music was part of my life. It stayed within easy reach, filling in much-needed words, easing my pain, and warning me of what could be just around the corner.

I should not be that close to a white person. I had been taught to always stay at a safe distance. On that particular day and at that particular time, while facing Camille's mother, Little Cliff felt I was out of the safe distance range.

It was she and not I who broke my uneasy silence.

"Mister Taulbert, my daughter here has told me so much about you. I must say that she was right. I came specifically to hear your talk."

As gracious as her words were, I was still taken aback. This was not what Little Cliff had been taught to expect. I had no choice other than to respond.

"Thank you so much, Miss Camille," I blurted without thinking.

I surprised myself. I knew her last name to be Sharp. Camille had introduced her to me. Even so, my Southern childhood kicked in and without hesitation I referred to her as "Miss Camille." This is what I would have done as a child back home. And just like back home, she accepted it as commonplace and continued talking.

"I certainly enjoyed it, every single word of it. You left us all with much to think about. Your people must be awfully proud of you with all that you have accomplished."

She did not avert her eyes even briefly; it felt that she was looking inside of me. This was all shaping up in unexpected ways. And the way she said that *my people must be awfully proud of me* was layered with levels of her understanding of the difficulties I must have faced. I could tell she understood that my walk from the Delta had not necessarily been easy. Yes, my people were proud of me because they knew firsthand the difficulty of being black in the South and moving beyond the cotton fields that sought to define our lives forever. My people knew I could have failed as so many of my peers did. The system that fueled our young lives was not designed for us to maximize our potential. Somehow I knew that this lady was fully aware of this. She continued talking directly to me as I balanced my present situation with my past.

"Now, Mister Taulbert, is this your first time in Allendale?" She was smiling as she talked, still holding onto my hand as a caring aunt might. Her demeanor and her gracious conversation contributed to making an afternoon of introspection for me. I even found myself analyzing how she had referred to me as "Mister Taulbert." Coming from her, the title of "Mister" took on an entirely different meaning that afternoon. It could easily have been described as her being politically correct in this college setting, but it didn't feel that way. As deep in the South as we were, I knew she meant it. It was quite obvious to me that we had both come from worlds where such respect was reserved for white men and their coming-of-age sons, not black boys or black men—not even black writers. I was appreciative and confused. At her age, why was she reaching beyond the social norms of her generation?

I felt as if everyone in the room had slowed down, and we were the center of attention, with the people—most of them my age—whom she had stopped, hugged, or patted on the hand analyzing every move. *Surely, she must have been a great schoolteacher in her time,* I thought to myself as I finally responded.

"Yes, ma'am, this is my very first time in Allendale."

"Do you like what you've seen of our country?" she asked, continuing to look me directly in the eyes. I noticed that she referred to her section of the world as "our country."

"Yes, ma'am. It's so hot, though."

"Why, of course, this is the South. We need the heat down here. This day, though, is record-breaking, but I was determined to get out and hear you."

"I'm glad you came. I have heard your name, but I never expected to meet you in person," I answered politely. But I was still ill at ease. I was feeling as if I had become two people: one a man of the twenty-first century and the other a boy who had never moved from his early life in the segregated South. What had started as a simple introduction was turning into an emotional walk down the dirt roads of the Delta.

She continued to talk unhurriedly, and her daughter just stood there smiling. I knew other people were waiting to talk with her, but there seemed to be no plans to whisk her away. And for me, as the conversation continued, I found myself feeling as if our paths had crossed before. I had never been to Allendale. And from what I could tell, she had never even heard of Glen Allan. As we talked about my speech and her South, I was participating, but my heart was in another place, torn by conflict and disoriented. I felt truly and sincerely welcomed, and that welcome also felt intimidating.

Finally, after stretching my imagination and memory as far as I could, I stopped turning pages in my memory—I knew her! We had not physically met, but emotionally our paths had crossed many decades ago, when I was a child. It was absolutely uncanny! She looked just like Miss Jeffries from back home, who owned Wildwood Plantation.

No wonder I was feeling uncomfortable touching this woman! To me, she *was* Miss Jeffries. I had worked in her cotton fields alongside my family and our friends, where the feeling of being intimidated and feeling less-than was part of the house of cards called segregation. That's how Miss Jeffries made us feel, and that's exactly who this lady now holding my hand and smiling into my eyes looked like. It made no sense to me that Camille's mom, no doubt a retired South Carolina educator, would evoke the memory of a plantation owner who, if alive, would be well over one hundred and fifty years of age.

But I was relieved be able to explain that unsettling sense of familiarity. Of course, I kept all of this in my head. I felt certain than none of this identity searching and matching would be of significance to anyone other than myself or another black person from my era. As the elder Camille continued to talk, I stood quietly attentive.

"You know, Mister Taulbert, my daughter told me about your talk in Columbia, which they all enjoyed, and of course, your lecture in Philadelphia. She said you brought the crowd to its feet. I can see why. Besides being a grand place to give a talk, Philadelphia is a wonderful city, you know . . . so much of our history there—the Revolution and all. Yes, my Camille came home and told me all about it—and you. After hearing her go on and on, I had to come and hear you myself."

I never thought Camille would have shared the Philadelphia story in such detail with her mother. Like me, I could tell that Miss Camille had great respect for that city. I had not thought about the response in Philadelphia for several years, but she was right. I had been overwhelmed at the response of that mostly white audience to my description of the unselfish life of the ordinary black people who had raised me. My "porch people" were and remain my heroes. They are the South I love. Growing up in Glen Allan and being relegated to an inferior position in life, I always felt overwhelmed and appreciative when others recognized my elders with the same level of respect as I did.

"I am delighted you came by," I told her. "I wondered why Camille left me up here alone."

"Someone must have run up and told her that I wanted to meet you before I had to leave. She didn't have to come and get me. I was on my way to the front, but I know just about everybody in Allendale. I guess with her help, I made it up here before they turned the lights off."

I watched as her face broke into a smile as she spoke about all the people she knew, her age, and how she dealt with it. We both laughed knowingly and she continued her conversation.

"I must say, it was worth my coming. It reminded me of so much. I enjoyed all you had to say, and especially the way you said it. Now, Mister Taulbert, do you expect to come back to Allendale?" Her question took me by surprise. By the tone of her voice, I could tell that she genuinely wanted an answer.

"Miss Camille, please call me Clifton. Now, my coming back all depends on how my lecture is accepted and your daughter's recommendation."

"Well, if that's all it takes, Mister Taulbert, you'll surely be coming back."

As we shook hands for the second time, I thought about the other black man that she had embraced earlier as if he were a grandson, and I thought about Miss Jeffries from Glen Allan. None of this should have mattered, but it all mattered to me. The lingering lessons of race and place are part and parcel of who I am. I accepted her praise without hesitation, but I also needed to understand why at first her presence reminded me of Miss Jeffries and made me feel that shaking her hand placed me too close to what had been off limits all my young life. I knew Little Cliff had to be confused with both the past and the present showing up at the same time.

I watched as she faded into the crowd, stopping and speaking to everyone as she left. This is the irony of my life, having to continuously deal with a world and a way of life that should have ended at Appomattox. Reaching beyond my relegated world has not been an easy task, just as it was troublesome to embrace Miss Camille's graciousness without hesitation. There's always that inner voice reminding me not to throw caution to the wind. Those lessons of race and place were powerful and indelible, and I am never too far from the world that shaped my early life. They are the burden of the past that I carry on my shoulders, as do so many others who made their way through the dark passageway of legal segregation.

I LEFT THE COLLEGE that afternoon knowing I had once again unashamedly brought my kin to dinner, but I also left with this older white lady on my mind. That moment in the auditorium talking with Miss Camille just would not go away. I found it difficult to forget all the past that my head had dealt with as we talked. I had not thought of Miss Jeffries in forty years or more. There was no reason to. I left home in 1963 committed to leaving the past behind, a past which included all the field hand labor I had done on Wildwood Plantation.

That evening, while resting in the hotel, parts of the afternoon continued to bother me. It was all so strange. However, I would be leaving the next day, and in all likelihood I would not be crossing paths with Miss Camille again.

Back in Tulsa, I told my wife about that uneasy afternoon in Allendale. Barbara listened, but I was unable to really convey what I had experienced. On the one hand I was trying to tell her about the graciousness I had experienced, and on the other hand about how unsettled Miss Camille's presence made me feel. The confusion still churned inside me and talking didn't help.

Our busy lives moved on, and I returned to my normal groove, preparing more lectures. But that unusual afternoon, the handshake, and the conversation between the black writer and the older white lady from Allendale continued to move in and out of my thinking.

Several months had passed when a small and dainty letter showed up in our mailbox. I can still see it in my hands as I walked from the mailbox back to the house. It was a small thank you-like envelope, ivory-colored, with my name and address written with an ink pen. I flipped the envelope over to see an unfamiliar street address in South Carolina nicely written on the back of the envelope. I laughed as I envisioned it being from Camille or the dean that I had met at the college in Allendale. But when I opened the handwritten note and raced to the bottom of the page to see who had signed it, I was taken by surprise. I yelled out to my wife.

"Barbara, you've got to see this."

"See what? Cliff, what are you yelling about?"

I was always accused of yelling. Barbara said my poor hearing was impacting my talking.

"This note from Miss Camille."

"Miss Camille? Who's that?"

"You know, the white lady that I tried to tell you about. The lady from Allendale, South Carolina—the one who held my hands, these black hands, and rather than just dropping them immediately held onto them and basically stared me down. Now I have this note from her right here in my hand. I wonder what she's saying?"

"Well, read the note!"

So I did, and as I read aloud, I was taken back to that afternoon, hearing Miss Camille's voice and seeing her face, just like before when it seemed as if we were the only two people in the world, an aging white lady and a "colored" boy from Glen Allan, onstage and observed by all those surrounding us. Although the experience was still with me, I never expected to see her again. I definitely never expected to hear from her. She had no reason to write me.

As I sat in my den reading her handwritten note, I tried to figure out why my conversation had meant so much to her. Obviously, given her age and retirement, as well as the fact that she was from a South that I thought I had left behind, this note was definitely unexpected. She thanked me once again for sharing my people with the audience in Allendale. It was all very gracious but made little sense to me, especially when Little Cliff kept thinking of her as Miss Jeffries from back home. Miss Jeffries was certainly not one to write a note of thanks to a black person. She might speak to the black visitor, yes, but would certainly not take the time to compose a handwritten note.

"I can't believe it," I told Barbara. "This note is very kind and warm, not at all what I would have expected from her."

"Clifton, people write kind notes, even white people."

I knew Barbara was right. My desk was filled with notes of thanks from people all over the world, and from all kinds of people. This note, however, was different. I wished that I could analyze her handwriting for a clue to explain all the questions that this simple, handwritten note raised. I wasn't a handwriting expert, and neither was Barbara, so Miss Camille's note joined the others in my desk drawer. But the conversation we held was not so easily laid to rest.

OVER THE NEXT FEW months, I continued traveling to conferences as part of my consulting work, speaking at schools, developing leadership workshops for businesses, and working with governmental agencies in Washington, D.C. I was determined to sidetrack as best I could the lingering lessons of race and place.

I had grown accustomed to being mistaken for a waiter and am always mentally prepared for that situation—not unlike what happened to me several years previously when I was an invited guest at the Alabama Shakespeare Festival, but several times throughout the evening was asked to provide drinks. My host, Professor Nancy Anderson, had been undone with embarrassment, and I had to ease her concerns. For me, it was just part of being black in America—this time in Montgomery, Alabama. I really understood the mistake. I was black. I was in a black tuxedo, and, historically, such a venue would have been closed to those who looked like me, except those serving as waiters. That's the daily challenge many professional African Americans of my era face; living in the present that is still shadowed by the past.

I know this to be true. When my paths cross with black professionals, I ask the proverbial question, "Hey, man, how's everything going?" The answer in many cases is, "Oh, man, it's the same old, same old." Nothing more needs to be said, since it is intuitive that issues of race exist and that they'll probably be there tomorrow. We have learned to live with that reality. We may talk a bit about it, but most often we simply move on, holding inside the conversations that are seeking a way out.

I could never bring myself to tell Camille how I felt while standing in the presence of her mother. It would have made no sense to her. At least that is what I thought.

The mere fact that I was there in an integrated group, and as the guest speaker, should prove that America and the South have moved on. In today's world—which admittedly is a far cry the world of my youth—it's difficult to acknowledge and explain the lingering lessons of race and place and how they continuously invade the consciousness of many Southerners like me. When I acknowledge them, am I extending the reach of the past into our present lives? When I keep quiet about them, am I appreciating the present, with its hope for the future, without stirring the pot? It is all so conflicting.

Legislation may have changed the laws and even created new possibilities for black Americans, but unfortunately, those laws were not able to scrub my personal and emotional hard drive and, I am sure, that of so many others.

Integration was intended to create the space where proximity between the races would highlight our shared humanity, thus alleviating many of the internal conversations about worth and value that continue to shadow many lives, especially for baby boomers like me. For many of us, integration was the conversation of promise, a way of life just around the corner. Despite the pending social changes that were promised, the Jim Crow laws that were predicated upon racial superiority and intimidation were still in place and practiced as if they were here to stay. That was the reality that sought to define my existence—the past that still shows up, even while you are dressed up.

Those old Jim Crow laws showed up in my head that day in Allendale while I stood with Miss Camille. I can only imagine the thoughts moving through the heads of our observers. Surely, to them, we looked like the repudiation of Jim Crow—the New South, two generations, one white and one black crossing a bridge together. From the outside, everything looked great, but no one in the audience actually knew what was going on in my head, nor in Miss Camille's.

To be the New South is to be a better America. It's about standing tall and with confidence to battle the ghosts of the past. It requires an intention to build a different and better place—and this is a process that many still find difficult to tackle. But I know "community" to be that place, as did Dr. Martin Luther King Jr., who wrote so eloquently about the "Beloved Community." That's what I saw my elders do. They built community to withstand the travesty of legal segregation and left their children with a clear picture of what was possible.

This is why my talks are so important to me. I don't want another generation of young men and women who should be steeped in the pursuit of excellence to still be saying, "Oh, man, it's the same old, same old." This is why I am so zealous about this unselfish and powerful process that can create lessons for our children that are unlike those lingering lessons that haunt my life.

I have had some of those better lessons, too, those worthy of remembering and passing along: memories like those I made while in the United States Air Force, where buddies like John Palozzi of New York, Jerry Williams of Alton, Illinois, and Paul Demuniz of Portland, Oregon—white boys, all three—squeezed into my life along with black friends like Orell Clay, Robuck, and Canty. Those guys left me with new pictures of how brotherhood could look. Many of us would take our military experiences into the rest of our lives, further impacting the maturity of America.

Without such memories of what is possible, it would be impossible for me to live a productive life. There would be too many memories like those that hit me in Allendale, continuously resurfacing and in some way slowing the process down.

Back home in Tulsa, and also when traveling to consult with clients in Belgium, Hong Kong, and Germany, I never forgot the unexpected impact of that afternoon in Allendale and the follow-up handwritten note, which I had carefully tucked away. But I kept my thoughts to myself and focused on my work in those places where no Southern dirt roads existed and where no gracious but emotionally intimidating Southern ladies appeared to remind me of the past.

World traveler though I had become, part of me had not moved too far from the days when my movement was defined by the color of my skin. I thought that I was in charge of my itinerary. As the months flew by, I would soon learn that I may have been in charge of my itinerary, but I was not in charge of providence.

5

An Unexpected Invitation

*"Nearly all the best things that came to me in life have been
unexpected, unplanned by me." —Carl Sandburg*

THE SUMMER OF 2001 WAS NO DIFFERENT THAN ANY OTHER
summer in Oklahoma. It was hot! That didn't matter, I had my schedule,
one which now included a visit to North Carolina in early September. South
Carolina and Allendale were not on my schedule.

I was excited. The North Carolina consulting opportunity had come
about as a result of my alignment with an international leadership development company, Ninth House. I was excited to work with Dan Hart again,
one of the lead team members at Ninth House at the time.

As September rolled around, the heat of summer began to give way to
a hint of fall. All the last-minute travel details were in place, and I made
ready to meet with Dan and the diversity team at Wachovia Bank to help
them understand the role that building community and the "eight habits
of the heart" could play in creating dynamic, inclusive teams, committed to
the mission of the bank and the needs of all their customers. I could hardly
wait for my day of travel on September 11, 2001.

Need I say more?

On that day of tragedy and chaos, I never made it to Charlotte where the
Wachovia meeting was to take place. I was among those million Americans
flying that day who found themselves wandering aimlessly through their

local airports trying to understand what had happened. Finally, through the tears and muddled words of a distraught fellow traveler in our Tulsa International Airport, I learned that the Twin Towers in New York City had been bombed. *Are we at war? What is going on? Is this the end of the world?* My head was filled with questions. In that moment, my life changed. Life in America changed. And I had no idea why.

Wachovia Bank was no longer a priority. As much as I had anticipated this professional opportunity, it was no longer on my mind. My thoughts immediately flashed to my teenage years to the first major tragedy of my generation, the assassination of President John F. Kennedy. That was a day so much like this one, with people walking around in shock. Back then, as we gathered at Saint Mark's Baptist Church in Glen Allan's colored section, we had the same unanswered questions. But at Saint Mark's, the unexplained was always met with a song. Troubled as I was, my elders in their own ways had seen more. Their souls would talk to each other in the music that permeated those old wooden plank walls. I found comfort then. I needed that same comfort on 9/11. I needed their songs of assurance that everything would be all right.

After Kennedy's assassination, I had been in the military during the ending days of the Vietnam War and I recall vividly how we were trained to go "overseas." With so many of my friends dying daily, I was beyond anxious for my call—a call that never came—to war overseas. That's where wars took place, overseas, not here at home.

On September 11, 2001, I had no reference for the tragedy unfolding on our home shores. For several months, apprehension invaded all our lives, while at the same time our shared humanity appeared to be more powerful than the social constructs that had governed many of our lives. Maybe we need such moments to uncover our better selves and remind us that we are on this journey together. In New York City and around America after 9/11, we were building community, the same type of community I had talked about with the people in Philadelphia, Columbia, and Allendale.

In the months following 9/11, I continued to lecture on the subject of community, taking people back to my hometown of Glen Allan and on some occasions referring to the tragedy and the sense of community that we witnessed as ash-covered Americans united on the streets of New York City, without regard to their normal barriers. The horrific incident had shown us a picture of sisterhood and brotherhood. We somehow found the strength and courage to make our way through the end of the year and through a Christmas and holiday season unlike any other I had known.

Seasons change and the calendar turns. With mustered strength and courage, we welcomed 2002, but without the usual fanfare. During those early days of 2002, 9/11 was ever present as we attempted to return to normalcy.

It was during that winter season, while focused on tax receipts and expense reports, that I received an invitation from Camille to return to South Carolina. Although much had happened in my life since that summer afternoon I spent there, I had been unable to place Allendale in the completed file. And now I was being invited back for the upcoming 2002 summer professional development programs. We would be working in small towns, none close to Allendale; this limited my opportunity of running into Camille's formidable mother, whose sheer presence affected my thinking.

The programs would deal with new strategies to bring sustainable positive behavior into the K-12 school environment. We all recognized that behavior mattered and that encouraging youth, wherever they are, to build community would be a good thing indeed. The 9/11 tragedy would provide a good starting place to point out what happens when a shared community is not present in our lives. The lack of community had become an international conversation. It appeared that for many humans around the world, our differences—rather than the gift of humanity we all shared—had become our mantra.

This was not unlike the world I knew as a child. In the South, we had majored in highlighting and pinpointing our differences. What better time than now to show this generation of young people the positive aspects of our shared life and to help them understand what can happen when we fail to make room for others to maximize their gifts? This would be my over-arching goal—to help the South Carolina educators understand and appreciate that their classrooms could become models for a shared democracy. I wanted a different future for this first generation of the new century. I didn't want them to be saddled with the same burdens that my generation was bearing as we tried to bridge the racial gulf that had been the way of life for generations.

Going back to South Carolina would let me offer its educators more concrete reasons why they should focus on building community as well as embrace this opportunity as a continuous process, not merely another project to check off. Needless to say, I accepted the invitation. Miss Camille and her note remained tucked away.

JUNE FINALLY ARRIVED AND I was off to the Low Country, anticipating the heat and humidity. Camille and Alan again met me at the airport. It was good to see them and catch up on their lives. After hugging each other and shaking hands and leaving the airport, our conversation in the car went immediately to 9/11 and its impact. Talking with them brought it all back as if it had just happened. Gradually the car went quiet as we pondered the time that had placed our national and personal mortalities right in our faces.

Suddenly, Camille changed the conversation, cheerily inserting information about her mother that I certainly hadn't expected.

"Mister Taulbert, Mama wanted you to know that she would not be able to make your training session. She was so looking forward to doing so. Now that she's retired she's busier than ever. Her fingers are in everything, and especially her church."

Though I did not express it to Camille and Alan, I was surprised that the elderly Miss Camille had sent me this message, and that she had considered attending. Something was happening beyond the ordinary as related to Miss Camille, but I had no idea yet what it could be.

"Thanks, Camille," I answered as casually as I could, "and be sure to pass my greetings along to your mother. It would have been nice to see her again."

"And she wanted to see you," Camille continued. "Mama is not known for taking to people as quickly as she took to you—and in just that one meeting." Camille smiled through the rearview mirror.

Took to me, I thought to myself. That was indeed a Southern term and was culturally weighted with stuff I understood but would find difficult articulating to others. Suffice it to say, she had looked beyond the obvious barriers and made her own decision. There was definite intentionality on her part.

But why me?

"Mister Taulbert, you know Mama took notes. Can you imagine, at her age, she was taking notes like some schoolgirl. Well, I had told her that she'd like your talk, and by God, I guess she did."

Even though our paths were not going to cross, Miss Camille Cunningham Sharp had somehow found her place inside this car and inside my head. As Camille expressed her surprise at her mother's "taking to me" as she had, I was doing likewise but staying silent on the subject. I could not bring myself to tell Camille that her mother's presence had in some way been very intimidating, hurling me back to my youth, to Wildwood Plantation and its fearsome owner, Miss Jeffries, who was part of the memories I wanted to forget. Instead, I sat quietly in the back seat, remembering her mother's parting words to me: *"I'm so glad that Camille found you and brought you to us. You'll be coming back."*

She was right. I was back. And I knew Miss Jeffries would not have been concerned about my return; then again, she would not have been at a place where I was speaking, either. In her day, our worlds were severely separated. It was the era of separate and mostly unequal. Miss Camille also had to know that world. Yet she wanted to know if I'd be coming back. Did I have something to say that she wanted to hear, or did she have a conversation for me?

As we continued to drive along, I thought about Miss Camille's note and wondered if Camille was aware of it. "By the way, Camille, I received a handwritten letter from your mother over the summer."

"A note from Mama! She hardly writes anyone anymore. Well, what did she say?"

"She wished me well and basically went over my lecture."

I still didn't know much about Miss Camille, but that afternoon and the follow-up note were saying something to all of us. What?

ARRIVING AT OUR WORK site, I was introduced to and paired with the team from Boston University that was working with educators throughout the state. Camille, of course, would be overseeing all that was taking place.

I focused totally on my work with the educators and the consultants, taking full advantage of how I knew community to be a powerful and transforming asset. I was still excited that Dr. Kevin Ryan, the founder of Boston University's Center for the Advancement of Ethics and Character, had invited me to add my "Building Community" conversation to their Character Building Modules. I knew this to be important to the adult educators and their students, especially the black students, many from rural areas not too dissimilar from what I knew as a child. The all-white team from Boston welcomed me, and I of course found myself again evaluating my gifts in light of theirs. In my youth, "whites" had established the standards—or at least this is what emanated from the lessons I had learned.

Over the summer of 2002, I traveled back and forth to South Carolina. By my second visit, our routine was set. I knew what was expected of me and set out to deliver my part of the program. However, this time, I would be not be chauffeured by Camille but by Dr. Karen Bohlin, the assistant director of Dr. Ryan's center. I knew Karen; we had met before. Still, the lessons of race and place were already orchestrating my thinking. Intellectually, of course, I was a well-traveled professional fully comfortable in the wider world and decades removed from Jim Crow segregation. But rural South Carolina's racist past, so similar to the Mississippi of my childhood, was crowding in. I doubted many African Americans in my situation would have been unaware of what I was feeling, and sure enough, Little Cliff was leading the conversation in my head: *I am not sure about riding through the South Carolina countryside with a white woman.*

Miss Camille came to mind again, and with her my memories of Miss Jeffries. My childhood surfaced, and all the racism I had seen. My professional musing had lost its place. Instead of preparing to talk about our common goal to make a difference in the perspectives of the educators and in the lives of the students they taught, my past dominated my thoughts.

Just as when in Miss Camille's presence and in the car with Camille and Alan, I found myself saying absolutely nothing about how I was feeling inside. I was simply hitching a ride—but one that Little Cliff would have done slightly differently.

I have no idea what internal lessons of race and place Karen may have had to deal with. My thinking just kept rolling down that one track: She was white, I was black. I was male, she was female. In my world, black men had been killed for much less. I could hear my elders' voices loud and clear:

"You walk now. You walk. I don't care how tired you git, don't you ever git in a car with a white woman."

This lesson of race and place had been drilled into our brains. In Glen Allan, there were those white men who took it upon themselves to make sure that those lessons were learned and practiced to the letter.

But here I was, riding "shotgun" with Karen. Then it got worse. I learned that the lodging for the team was in at a hunting camp—not a bed and breakfast or a hotel, of which there are hundreds, maybe thousands, throughout South Carolina, but a hunting camp. Why hadn't Camille thought of the social implications and the potential stress for me?

Despite Little Cliff's terror, we finally made it to our backwoods destination. It was night and very dark, and I gave a loud sigh of relief as we parked the car. The voices in my head quieted now. A single light bulb was burning on the front porch to welcome us. I laughed to myself. It looked just like the single-bulb porch light that used to welcome Little Cliff home to Mama Ponk's house.

The group was glad to see us and after some late night small talk—none of which touched on all the conversations in my head—the ladies retired to the main cabin to sleep and we guys headed off to one of the small outer cabins.

Once more, Little Cliff was uneasy.

I am the only black person sequestered out here in the woods with these white people—and maybe white hunters in other cabins. White men with guns.

THE NEXT MORNING WE had breakfast, packed our gear and headed to our next professional development assignment, working with more South Carolina K-12 educators. Needless to say, our work was well-received. Camille had been right about one thing, my conversations on community, and how a good and inclusive community could look going forward, were welcomed with more enthusiasm than I had dared imagine.

Like academic nomads, we were off to the next academy assignment, again driving through the South Carolina countryside. This time Karen's car carried several of us, including one of the white guys. Little Cliff was more at ease with this and, quite frankly, so was I.

While driving to the next academy in Florence, South Carolina, someone mentioned Camille's mother, Miss Camille, and how agile she was for her age. I listened and smiled inside, not adding anything to the conversation.

It had been over a year since our paths crossed. Even so, our meeting still filled my head with questions to which I had no answers. It was just so strange how her presence made me feel—as if I were a little boy, still living in the world of my youth, unchanged.

Our academy work in Florence went well. My hunting camp bunkmates from Boston continued to do a great job. They were out of their accustomed environment, being this deep into the South, but their hearts' desire to share knowledge with others more than made up for the trouble of living outside their usual comfort zone. In some small way, we were using our talents to make a better America by giving educators tools to build great learning environments while creating good relationships. With the end of this last summer academy, my friends headed home to Boston and New Hampshire, and I returned home to Tulsa.

Toward the end of 2002, I was notified that the summer academies would continue in 2003, funded by South Carolina's State Department of Education. Boston University was invited back, and I was included. When I got word of the travel arrangements, I breathed a great sigh of relief. Camille and Alan would be picking me up in Columbia. I had no desire to test the outcome of the civil rights movement a second time by once again riding alone with a white woman. I really liked Alan, and could hardly wait for one of our engaging international conversations. And, I was delighted to be returning.

As fate would have it, Camille and Alan were again unable to pick me up. I would be driven to the workshop by Mike and Dr. Kathy Paget. Kathy was one of the ladies I had first met in the lobby of the hotel in Philadelphia.

The June date came rather quickly. The Pagets met me at the Columbia airport. Kathy and I hugged. I was introduced to her husband, and we shook hands before making our way to the airport parking lot. We threw my stuff in the trunk, and I piled into the back seat. I was glad to be in the car. I was ready to go. Besides being really hungry, I couldn't wait to go to the restroom, something I should have done at the airport, but I figured I could wait until we got to the restaurant or to my hotel, which I wanted to be the Hilton or the Marriott—places I knew. So I kept my fingers crossed for the downtown Hilton. It was not far from the airport.

As we drove, we got busy talking and catching up on our respective sons, Marshall and Chris, who were about the same age. I didn't notice when we kept driving right through the city and past the Hilton Hotel. In fact, Kathy was not slowing down for supper or the bathroom. I deeply regretted having failed to exercise that option while in the airport.

Maybe we are headed to a new restaurant or something on the outskirts of town. But that was not the case. With the skyline of Columbia now almost out of sight and no restaurant signs in view, my concern got the best of me as well as my need to visit the men's room. I raised my head up, leaned over, and gently tapped Kathy's husband, Mike on the shoulder.

"Mike, what fancy restaurant do you have up your sleeve for supper?"

Before Mike could answer, Kathy chimed right in.

"Restaurant? Clifton, didn't Doug give you the last email?" Doug, my assistant, was usually on top of everything, but somehow this new and informative email had slipped through the cracks.

"Supper is all planned, and we're going to join the others at Camille's place," Kathy said with great excitement.

"Great, I've been by there once before. I can't wait to see Alan again," I said.

"Well, I'm not sure he'll be there," Kathy casually responded.

"Sure he will. He loves his gardening and watching things grow. Besides we have a couple of unfinished conversations. He knows so much about the Middle East and oil and all the culture of that world."

"I am sure you guys will eventually catch up on your conversation, but

I don't think it'll be today. He's not much for crowds and prefers the quietness of his home."

"We aren't that noisy, are we? If it gets to be too much for him, he can just go into his study and shut us out."

"Clifton, you are missing it. We won't be at Camille's and Alan's house."

"I thought you said we were having supper at Camille's place."

"I did, but I was referring to her childhood place. We'll be at Roselawn for supper. That's her mother's home."

"Oh, I see," I said as nonchalantly as possible. "You know I met her a while back when speaking at the college in Allendale."

"She's some lady, I understand," Mike chimed in.

"I must say that her personality defies her size." I quickly added, but said nothing more about how our one meeting had gone three years before, and how I had felt diminished in stature while in her presence. The news that we were now headed to Miss Camille's came as a surprise to me. All I could think about was that I certainly didn't want to relive the meltdown of returning to my segregated childhood.

"Roselawn," I said, "is that the neighborhood where their place is located?"

Kathy chuckled. "Well, Clifton, it's not the name of a neighborhood."

"Then what is it? Seems like I heard Karen call it their farm or something, right?"

Kathy looked at me through the rearview mirror. "It's not really a farm, Clifton, not like we tend to think of farms," she answered with thoughtful, measured words.

"Then what is it? A peach orchard? They have peaches growing on every patch of ground 'round here."

"Clifton, Camille's family farm is really something a bit more substantial, wouldn't you say so, Mike?"

"I guess you could say 'substantial' is the right word."

"Okay, so what are you saying?"

"Clifton, it's an antebellum Southern plantation. They don't grow peach trees. They grow cotton—thousands of acres of cotton."

Silence settled within the car.

Little Cliff had not been mistaken when I looked at Miss Camille in that auditorium in Allendale and saw Miss Jeffries, owner of Wildwood Plantation, where I had picked cotton as a child. Now I was headed back there, it seemed. Invited to supper.

My elders had no songs for such an invitation. An invitation to Beulah land, yes—but none for this. I *needed* a song. I needed one badly, but all the hymns and blues and gospel melodies that sustained Little Cliff in childhood had flown. The church was closed. No one was at the piano. The juke joint was not open and the Seeburg was unplugged. And the voices in the fields had been silenced.

I can't explain why, but somehow all the history associated with the word "plantation" had drowned out everything else. My path has taken me near plantation homes before. I see them every time I go back home to Mississippi—a permanent reminder of who was once "boss" in so many lives. Today, however, it had taken on an entirely different feeling as I tried to put all the pieces of my forming puzzle together. At least I now knew that Miss Camille was no retired schoolteacher. Her powerful presence was beginning to make some sense.

It was obvious that Mike and Kathy were well aware of the implications of the Southern plantation in the history of my life, from slavery to sharecropping. The issues of race and place had to be running through all our minds. How could they not? We all knew exactly what this was all about. Southern plantations and their gracious ways of living, built upon the backs and labor of slaves, were known by all. Plantation life had been memorialized in movies and in books by great writers. The antebellum South had indeed been a world unto itself—the world of "them and us."

In the silence, an emotional heaviness settled over me. I felt as if I were now bearing the whole weight of being black in America upon my shoulders. We were all thinking, but not talking. The subject remains a difficult one in America, no matter the conversationalists. I knew I could not change history.

Finally, Kathy broke the silence. "Clifton, Camille's family's history goes way back before the Civil War. Their home is listed on the National Historic Register. Her mother even gives tours of the family home."

I was silent again, but familiar warning voices, like torrents of rain, filled my head—not one small voice, but many voices all at once. I knew those voices well. For most of my adult life, they had reminded me that the lessons of race and place from my childhood lingered. These voices told me to be careful or else those constraints would be trying to define my life as they once had. Something deep inside me knew more than I could see on the surface. Although I hadn't at the time, Little Cliff had immediately recognized Miss Camille for a plantation owner and understood the power of her presence.

In my heart, I now knew that this would be no routine invitation to supper. Maybe routine for Mike and Kathy, but hardly so for me. I wasn't even at the plantation yet, and already uneasiness settling upon me like a big overcoat. And Camille, the daughter, had never let on. She gave no hint that her life was an integral part of the history of South Carolina, of the South, and of the role of the plantation system in enslaving generations of African Americans.

At some other time, such a dinner invitation might have been considered a coup—validating the Selma March or the great March on Washington—but not this time. Too many pictures of what had divided the races kept raining down upon me. I may have been in South Carolina in 2003, but the life I knew from the Mississippi Delta in the 1950s was crowding into the back seat, almost suffocating me. I bore this reality alone. Never once did I call upon my friends to come to my rescue. Once again, I felt myself shrinking emotionally, clearly reminding me of how we had learned to minimize our humanity while in the presence of whites. We were taught to never look a white person in the eyes. We were taught to always look away, or look down.

It was that feeling of shrinking that really bothered me. I recognized it. I hated it. How could the past be so powerful that it almost changed one's perspective of who one really is? I felt as if I were fighting to be the adult I had become. My mere presence in the car should have been all the validation I needed, but I needed more. I needed the memory of being a welcomed guest in the lives of others, and not just as labor. The past that had so successfully defined my coming-of-age years seemed determined to keep me undervaluing myself. It was as if all that I had accomplished would never be enough to feel fully welcomed in the "big house." Those were the places that stood as physical reminders of the difference in race and color.

I could feel Mike's and Kathy's eyes through the rearview mirror. I wouldn't look up. I didn't want our eyes to meet. At that moment, they would not have seen the sparkle and the brightness that many say defines me. And anyhow, what could they say? They could be sympathetic, but they were white. There's no way they could understand me feeling smothered by the way of life I once had to live, playing like an old-time movie in my head.

Standing in line at the post office and being told to step back when a white person walked in . . . the stark differences in our homes . . . the stinging remarks that reminded me I was not allowed to play in the park.

I had not expected to see Miss Camille again, and now I wasn't sure how I would respond. She turned out to be what Little Cliff had suspected all along, a far cry from retired schoolteacher role I had given her. And her home would not be a typical South Carolina bungalow.

My mind was in overdrive trying to deal with the big divide of race, place and class—a chasm that seemed to have been growing bigger by the minute. Soon to face Miss Camille's plantation, another plantation memory was in the meantime knocking at my door, this time from Natchez, Mississippi, another Southern town that is known for its preservation of the antebellum lifestyle. It was on the grounds of Natchez's Melrose Plantation that I was almost brought to tears as I saw clearly the world of the slaves.

I HAD COME TO Natchez as a guest writer to talk to a group of prominent Americans and their equally prominent guests, gathered from across the country, as part of an outing sponsored by the Bohemian Club, an exclusive men's club located outside of San Francisco. I was one of several invited Southern writers, including Shelby Foote and John Barry, all of us at various waterway ports to talk about our specific Southern experience. The Port of Natchez, and specifically Melrose Plantation, a majestic antebellum home, was my site. Melrose was built in the early nineteenth century by John T. McMurran, a Philadelphia lawyer, as a gift for his wife, Mary Louisa, and was a monument to the Old South if ever there was one.

Unlike Roselawn, Melrose was no longer a functioning plantation—no invitations to suppers there. It belonged to the National Park Service and was a magnificent home that seemingly appeared out of nowhere when I first saw it the morning I was scheduled to speak. As we made our way through a line of trees laced with hanging moss, I could see the majesty of the house from the tour bus windows and could only imagine the splendor that would be inside. It was breathtaking. For a while, I was an engrossed spectator, like all the rest.

However, when we departed the bus and followed the tour guide into the home, I was overwhelmed with thoughts about the people who would have been part of the building process of such a grand home at such a time in history. Inside the grand home, there was no physical evidence of slavery, and it was not part of the tour guide's conversation, but I felt slavery all around me. When this was a functioning home for its owners, black hands would have been intimately involved in all aspects of the labor, from hanging the framed portraits we were admiring to polishing the silver and waxing the wooden floors. Without the working presence of our brothers who were slaves, such homes would not have been possible.

Many of the rooms were roped off from visitors, further marking a historical era that had ended yet quietly and elegantly extended its presence into the twenty-first century. It was thought-provoking—more grandeur than I had ever seen, even considering all my travels throughout Europe. The furniture was massive, elegantly and painstakingly carved and had been kept immaculate by the efforts of the house slaves. The best of Europe had been imported to this wooded frontier to create a place of comfort where I would never have been a guest. My "place" would have already been decided by my color, as had been the "place" of those who looked like me when this grand home was their workplace.

The reality of Melrose became exceedingly clear as I exited the elegance indoors and made my way outside. That is when I saw my "place," the place of my people, the carefully restored slave cabins located on the very edge of the manicured grounds. The place where the slaves lived was called the "quarters," but they were almost hidden from view by the hedge of trees that separated the lawn of the mansion from the start of the fields that bordered the quarters. They were almost out of view, maybe deemed by the restorers as unnecessary to the story of the South. They were far enough away not to encumber the beauty of the mansion and close enough to be well within the sound of the massive bell that called slaves to work. I needed no park guides to tell me that what I was seeing would have been my world had I lived during that era.

There was nothing substantial about the slave cabins. No thought had gone into the design. There was no intricate woodwork to admire. Cracks in the walls and floors were still obvious where the outside would have come inside uninvited. By contrast, much thought had gone into every nail hammered and every plank assembled at the Melrose mansion. Melrose was a home, a place where people could dream about their future and the future of their children.

The cabins, though, reminded me of a shed where equipment was stored or prized animals would be sheltered from the weather. With both pictures in my head, the division between the owners and the slaves was physically poignant. As I looked at the contrast between "them and us," I understood how easy it would have been to grow up without a sense of self, while around them others would grow up with a very high opinion of themselves.

I'll never forget the feeling of powerlessness that came over me as I thought about those who were human like me, but had no power over their own lives. And I never knew a home could be so small.

With such thoughts running through my head, I feared I would be unable to stand in front of the all-white crowd and take them on the journey to my small hometown, where my elders had somehow managed to beat the odds on my behalf. At Melrose Plantation, the imported and home-grown slaves were long gone, but the insidious reach of that world still shadowed Glen Allan generations later and had been awaiting me at my birth. Of course, also awaiting at my birth was the nurturing of my elders that I received and will always cherish. The slave cabins took me back to the sharecropping life that had been ours, and to the people who had made my life bearable. That day I loved the elders even more as I thought about the difficulties they faced simply because they were black. In spite of my books and the prominent place waiting for me at the podium this day, at my core I was one of them. I remembered that in my childhood my color had dictated my station in life as surely as it had that of my elders and the slaves who had come before them.

Seeing those slave shacks and realizing what they were, I purposely moved away from the crowd. I had to make my way from the laughter and the commentary about the structure of the mansion and its well-kept grounds. Their conversation was not mine. We didn't have the same story and nowhere was it more obvious than at Melrose Plantation. I was the guest speaker, the black author who had escaped the clutches of the culture that had surrounded my early life. I was an example of what is possible in America. I was all of that, but so much more. I was also kin to the slaves who had lived at Melrose. This reality took precedence over the fact that I was surrounded by some of the most important people in America.

I had been captured by my past. As I could hear the others' laughter and chatter, I could also feel tears of pity, anger, and humiliation welling up inside of me. Should I start to cry, I didn't want them to see me. I can tell you that during those moments, I felt alone. I slowly walked away, across the lawn, needing some personal time and a place to wipe my eyes. I wanted to reflect on my people who had been left with no choice about their future; human beings forced to live beneath their gift of humanity just to satisfy a way of life for others, a way of life with greed at its core.

At first glance, I wanted to pass the slave quarters without too close a look. Perhaps this was the time to just move on, as if slavery was a story in a history book. It's conceivable that, in that crowd, others may have been having their own turns of thought. Like me, they could very well see how the great divide had looked, and perhaps better understand what it had cost America. I'll never know, because no such conversation was held between them and me.

Just observing the cabins' exteriors caused more feelings to surface than I could handle. The whitewashed and faded wood-framed shacks were ghostly and uninviting, a sure sign that we had not mattered. Had I walked on by with the crowd, I would not have had to deal with the humiliation and hurt welling up inside of me. I didn't walk on by, though. I mustered the courage to pull one of the park rangers aside and request permission to go inside one of the cabins.

I didn't know what to expect . . . artifacts, furniture, the slaves' tattered clothes strewn across the bed? These small, hut-like houses were not replicas, were not constructed on a Hollywood set, were not photographs on a page that one could quickly turn. This is where my people actually lived.

These cabins were their homes, where they made their children, cooked their food, and suffered.

The ranger immediately agreed to let me see the interior of the slaves' quarters. Quietly and by myself, I slowly walked into my history. I had to bend low to enter the front door, so unlike the massive carved doors that welcomed us into the nearby mansion. The interior of the slave shack was even smaller than I had expected. I had problems standing to my full height. Here were no high ceilings with intricate carvings connecting the walls and the ceilings. Here were no ornate framed photographs on the walls of well-dressed men and women. Here were no silk ball gowns draped across the foot of the bed, no fine china to touch, and no fancy dining table to see. Here was no imported carpet. This floor was bare and worn. I was not in the "big house" for sure!

I closed my eyes and tried to imagine the daily reality of living in this little house. It was hard to do. I remembered the home where I grew up, our two rooms for a whole family. It was no certainly no mansion, but the slaves who lived and worked this plantation had been worse off. For them, privacy did not exist. So bare was the room, I couldn't even fantasize a better life for them.

In every sense of the word, these were my kinfolk. They had suffered slavery. Some had survived the torturous transatlantic slave journey, the worst of which may never really be known. We can't truly imagine the cruelty they suffered in the bowels of Portuguese slave ships commanded by men who thought little or nothing of their lives. From those transatlantic journeys, the life of the slave was bequeathed to them; from there, a lifestyle that eventually became the life of legal segregation that I knew as a child. This is the legacy that shadows me, a way of life that my generation of baby boomers was charged to remodel as we passed through.

Back home in our small house in Glen Allan, we did share laughter. We looked to a different future. Human aspiration was present. I found it difficult to imagine laughter in the slave quarters. In the small cramped home of my childhood, we studied and thought about a better life. Such thinking would have been of no value in these slave quarters; their occupants belonged to someone else, and so did their future.

This was my experience at Melrose.

Now, A FEW YEARS later, and hundreds of miles from my small hometown, I found myself being invited from the fields to supper at Roselawn Plantation, a type of place that was, to me, symbolic of the worst of our times. Sitting in the back seat of Kathy and Mike's car, I could feel the weight of Melrose's world of masters and slaves, that indescribable feeling of being linked to a people and a time that was branded by human bondage. No matter how successful my life becomes, the reality of my American journey will always be marred by the fact that my people were once owned. I cannot just toss this reality to the winds of history and move on. Once again I was feeling the "place" that society had assigned me. I am sure that Mike and Kathy were sympathetic. But without the emotional reality that was mine alone, there would be little they could do to ease my pain.

Whereas for many, such a trip into history—being a guest at this Roselawn home—would have been a welcome experience. I felt it was for Mike and Kathy. But it was not so for me. This was not a field trip. I would have no need to take pictures. My head was already swirling with pictures, none of which I wanted to process and frame. I was in the twenty-first century, but my head was in the past, wondering how Roselawn and its people would have looked and behaved a century and a half earlier.

Roselawn was on the National Register of Historic Places, Kathy had said. But I didn't need to see another set of restored slave cabins. What I had seen in Natchez would last my lifetime. I had no desire to hear more about the glorious past of the Europeans who had forged through the wilderness, tamed the land, and created a legacy through their indomitable human will.

I could only think of the abominable system of slavery that had dehumanized my kin and the subsequent legal segregation that had passed slavery's vestiges along to my generation.

Slavery is not a legacy to be treasured and it has not been a topic I felt comfortable discussing freely. It was a way of life I wish had never been. Now this invitation to supper at Roselawn was taking me back to that world, and in a way I had not planned. Unlike at Melrose Plantation, I couldn't just walk in and look around and walk out with a handful of four-color brochures. No, this was Camille's family home, the place where her mother still resided.

My mind had journeyed all the way to Natchez and back, but in real time only seconds had passed in the car with Mike and Kathy. The conversation required a response from me.

"This is not what I expected." Those were the only words that came out of my mouth. Mike and Kathy were still quiet as I finally added, "I had no idea that she was a plantation owner. I thought she was a retired schoolteacher or something like that. Why didn't somebody tell me this earlier? I can tell you, it took me right back to Melrose."

"Melrose? What's that?" Mike asked, turning to face me.

"Oh, it's another Southern plantation."

I really didn't want to go into what had happened at Melrose, though I had just relived every bit of it and its impact on me was still real and raw. Maybe this would have been a good time to just lay my soul bare. The afternoon demanded the Bill Clinton-John Hope Franklin type of conversation. I just couldn't bring myself to discuss it. I didn't want to explain how the system of slavery was still reaching into the twenty-first century and personally impacting me. But Mike had asked a question, so I had to say something more.

"Plantations, no matter where they are, give me reasons for concern, if only historical. You know, growing up in the South and all."

"I see," Mike quietly responded.

"So Miss Camille is into cotton." I tried to be as casual as one could, when I really wanted to blurt out much, much more about cotton, race, slavery, integration, segregation, and just about every other race-related subject.

"She follows a long line of a prominent South Carolina family," Kathy added matter-of-factly.

I leaned forward onto the back of the front seat as we talked. "I knew something was different about her when we first shook hands and talked at the college that afternoon."

"Different?"

"First, I was taken with the way people fell all over her. That's when I assumed that she was a beloved schoolteacher. People were in waves trying to touch her."

"Oh, Clifton, it wasn't like that—was it?"

"I can see that," Mike replied to Kathy. "Camille's mother is a heavy-weight. I am surprised that Clifton didn't know all of this. He's been around here for a few years."

I said, "A historical antebellum connection never once crossed my mind. I couldn't imagine the daughter of a plantation owner chasing me down in the lobby of a Philadelphia hotel. Besides, I had seen Alan and Camille's home in Allendale. Nice, but modest. I wonder why Camille kept this from me."

"That's just Camille. She's not one to trade on her Southern pedigree."

"I admire that. But I still couldn't figure why her small-statured mother impacted me the way she did when we met. While standing there with everybody looking on, I was at a loss trying to second-guess my mind."

"What are you talking about?"

"Oh, Kathy, it's just something I have to deal with. I knew something was different about Camille's mother. Although we had never met, she re-minded me of someone from my childhood. I just couldn't figure out who it was. Finally, after going through the pictures in my mind of all the white women her age that I could recall, it hit me like a ton of bricks."

"So who did she remind you of?" Mike asked.

"A white plantation owner from Glen Allan, lady named Miss Jeffries. I have no idea of her first name. All the people, white and black, just referred to her as Miss Jeffries—even today after she's been deceased for decades. Miss Camille even looked like Miss Jeffries. This was a lady I had not thought of in decades. There had been no reason to."

After I described Miss Jeffries in detail, Mike and Kathy nodded their amazement at the similarities with Miss Camille. However, I was the one bearing the burden of the resemblance and feeling like a little "colored" kid again when in her presence. I didn't want to have that experience again. Maybe I should have expressed my swirling emotions. Instead, I just kept quiet.

As we drew closer to the plantation, Kathy continued framing Camille's childhood world.

"Clifton, the mansion is surrounded by beautiful fields of cotton. Young cotton plants are everywhere. Just wait, you will see." Kathy probably had no thought that cotton fields might not seem beautiful to me, but went on to tell me about her first visit to Roselawn.

Nor was Mike grasping my internal issues. He seemed determined to make up for the education I had missed. "Clifton, we'll have to go through a line of tall pine trees and a few big oaks covered with Spanish moss to get back to where the mansion is located. It'll make you think of one of those old Southern movies where, at the end of this tree-lined dirt road, this imposing structure emerges for all to see. It is like going back in time."

Going back in time was the last thing I wanted to do. I felt as if I was already back to my childhood. I needed desperately to move to a different place in my head. Forward, not back. As they talked about the grandeur of the home and grounds, my head was ahead of them.

I wonder who's working all the land? I know they are black people. It's always us.

I wanted to say this out loud, but I couldn't. As I thought about those days when I was working the fields and when black bodies bent or kneeled as far as the eye could see in the baking sun, I could feel anger rising inside. From the time I was five years old until I was in my late teens, the Mississippi Delta's fields were part of my life. I didn't want to see another cotton field, ever. But I was a writer, not an angry black man. So I kept quiet as I remembered how the Melrose tour guides were so excited to take us into that opulent world of the owners, but not into the cruel world of the slaves. Slavery and its aftermath were so horrible that maybe no one knows how to bring this searing history into our daily conversation.

I thought about the significant role South Carolina had played in moving Africans deeper into Southern states like Mississippi. Many of my kin passed through the Carolinas, through one of the ports where the slave-laden ships landed. From there, the human inventory was branded and shipped further south. I had learned about this part of our family's journey from my cousin Matthew Page, a retired doctor in Greenville, Mississippi. He had become a historian of sorts by necessity. From him, we learned about our family's connection to the cotton and rice lands of South Carolina, which could very well be some of the same land now owned by Camille's family. I was finding it difficult to be excited by an invitation to supper at a place that evoked such memories. And to think that Miss Camille, the lady who warmly held my hand while we talked, was linked to all of this.

Mike's conversation had trailed off. I guess my silence left little reason to keep talking. Quiet filled the car. Only the sound of the motor could be heard. Kathy looked straight ahead, while Mike took in the scenery surrounding us. I don't know how long we drove in this strange quiet, but finally Mike's Southern voice broke through the silence.

"Clifton, I can assure you that the food at Camille's place will be better than any restaurant in South Carolina. You're gonna be in for a real treat."

As much as I love to eat, eating was the last thing on my mind. However, before I could respond, Kathy chimed in.

"I couldn't agree more," she cheerily replied. "I have eaten there several times and trust me—it's top drawer," she answered with a type of perky assurance geared to keep that line of talk going.

I know I answered them, but I have no memory of what I said. What I must have been thinking at the time was *the food should be good. The black cook prepared it. We can't socialize with the whites, but they can't wait to eat the food we cook.*

I was on my way with them to supper, but my mind was still picturing the plantation life I remembered from the Delta: palatial homes with pillars that seemed to be reaching for the sky where great meals were prepared by the hands of the black help—delicious meals meticulously prepared for the owners. Those who prepared the mouth-watering meals were more often than not offered the leftovers, if anything at all, to take back to their small overcrowded shotgun houses. Even back then, the reputation of the black cooks was a topic of conversation. Why would it be any different at Roselawn Plantation?

FOOD MAY HAVE BEEN a great topic to break the silence, but the quiet soon came back, and with it, the lingering memories of race and place that defined my life. At that moment, I wanted to go back to Columbia, or anywhere but Allendale.

Quietly sitting in the back seat and looking out the windows was not helping. I saw the familiar scenes again: shirtless black children playing and running in the sun, rolling old tires as if they were massive trucks. It was as when I was in the car with Camille and Alan the first time I came to Allendale, further reminding me of the great social divide that still remained. I was afraid to close my eyes. I didn't want to dream about Glen Allan and Miss Jeffries's cotton fields.

Although I was feeling the impact of the past, I also realized that life had not passed me by. In fact, life had been good to me. While a young soldier during the Vietnam era, I was sent to the 89th Presidential Wing in Washington instead of to some remote place outside of Saigon where so many of my friends died. It was during this challenging time in my life that I started to write, with no idea that one day what I had written at night in a cramped barracks would become the book that would captivate talk show host Phil Donahue, or that I would meet former Supreme Court Justice Sandra Day O'Connor and be invited as her guest to share my story with members of the court and their guests at the Library of Congress. This, too, was my reality.

However, hearing about the plantation, seeing small black kids rolling tires, and picturing Miss Camille as Miss Jeffries were overshadowing everything else. I wanted this unfolding of my childhood to stop. I had no such luck; the past kept coming at me, taking me back home, back into the small, flowery-wallpapered bedroom that I shared with my great-aunt, Mama Ponk. I could smell her Garrett Snuff. I could see her, hair tightly wrapped in a scarf to ward off a bad cold, sitting in her rocking chair by the front window where she looked out and watched her world pass, and telling me to watch out for the town's white bully whose parents owned one of the small grocery stores uptown. I could see my great-grandfather, Poppa Joe, as I rode with him in his 1949 Buick, pulling up alongside the local gas station, making sure that he had not mistakenly blocked a white person. I could hear him giving me one more lesson of race and place.

"Go round the back and tap on the window. Just tap one time. Miss Bea can serve you if ain't no white people looking, she'll look your way. If she can't, she'll just shoo you away. You got that?"

I had moved past all this, but not really. My hard drive had captured every incident, and every incident of race and place was now present in the Pagets' back seat. I couldn't turn around and go back as much as I wanted to do so. I was not in control. It wasn't my car.

Kathy interrupted the silence. "Clifton, we are almost there. Camille's childhood home is just beyond that upcoming grove of trees."

My heart sank further. I remembered what Mike had said. My head was filled with multiple images of what I could expect to see. I kept quiet. Plus, with my head so preoccupied, I had forgotten how badly I needed to use the restroom.

Kathy's quick turn from the blacktopped road threw me back for a second, but I was fine. I swayed a bit as she turned sharply onto a dirt-packed road, another familiar sight from my childhood. Even the packed-in tire tracks looked familiar. Mike was right. I was indeed going back in time. The dirt road itself was reminiscent of every old dirt road I had known. The towering oak trees were laden with Spanish moss and the pines were so tall and the foliage so full that they hid the sun. The Old South was before me. Instead of gardens full of well-kept flowers, I saw the many acres of growing cotton. I saw my own yesterdays stretched across the fields as if I had just gotten off Mr. Walter's field truck.

And there it was—the mansion, the home of Miss Camille, where I had received an invitation to have supper. There were no towering white pillars like Melrose. Roselawn's mansion had an elegant simplicity that blended with the landscape as if the earth had been formed around it. I would later learn that such homes were called Low Country mansions. And to add to the conversations in my head, Miss Camille's home was identical to the design of Miss Jeffries's plantation home back in Glen Allan. The only difference was the size. Roselawn was much, much bigger! All of my earlier thinking was now coming together. I wasn't crazy, as I had sometimes thought when reflecting on that afternoon almost two years earlier when I first met Miss Camille. It was making sense, though I had yet to fully understand all that I would encounter and all that it would mean.

I could not stop staring. The mansion was this magnificent wooden structure that looked a bit weather worn, but historically elegant nonetheless. Time had not disturbed it. It left the impression that the Civil War never happened and that the landed gentry were still in control. There was no doubt of its antiquity. Tall windows with glistening panes looked out on every side. The shiny tin roof, the only part of the mansion that looked like part of the twenty-first century, was tall and pitched, giving it a majestic look, even more so as the remaining rays of the sun danced upon its surface. The long porch wrapped almost around the mansion, and the steep steps from ground to porch added grandeur.

I viewed all of this from the backseat of the Pagets' car. However, I remained ill-at-ease, thoughtful, and definitely apprehensive as Kathy excitedly broke the silence.

"Clifton, just like I told you, this antebellum place is something else. Can you imagine growing up here? Look at the flowering plants all around the house. Have you seen such flowers before? It's a magazine cover."

I was not thinking about *Southern Living* magazine. The cotton fields were still drawing my attention. Whenever I saw such a field while driving along a Southern route, I shuddered. It was not remembering hard work that caused my dread, but the culture around the work, and how we were treated as if we were human machines, toiling day-in and day-out, barely making a living, but with little choice for something different. For generations, the planters and their cotton fields had formed a grip that was hard to break. Many died never knowing that a new day would come.

Anxiety now overshadowed any logic I might have had left, and I became very concerned over whether I would be a welcome guest *here*, of all places. True, I was officially on the guest list, although I had missed the email. Still, I can assure you that my internal hard drive was working overtime, replaying the voices inside my head. Maybe I should have shared my feelings with Mike and Kathy, but I didn't.

I shouldn't be here. Who are the other guests? I bet they are all white. Maybe I'll know some of them from last year. They seemed pretty progressive, but you never know. We were at a college then, but this place is so different.

My emotions were in turmoil. There was no way I could come across as an accomplished writer or world traveler. The lingering lessons of race and place were altering my persona.

I thought of what Miss Camille had said almost two years earlier, "Your folks should be awfully proud of you." Was this invitation a reason to be proud of me? I don't know. In my folks' world, the possibility that I would one day have supper in the "big house" probably never crossed their minds. What could I do that would make them proud?

I know one thing for certain. For them, being successful meant that their children would never have to pick cotton again. They hated being relegated to the fields. They knew it was demeaning and demanding, but they had no choice. They had to make a living. They wanted us to get an education. They clearly understood its value and did all they could to make it accessible to us. They saw education as the ticket out of the fields.

I had not let them down, but as the Pagets' car approached Roselawn, I felt internally as if I had not achieved a single thing. I felt the weight of being "colored" and all it entailed. The liberation of civil rights legislation had not been able to take away the "mark" that branded us. I was black! In many ways I had lived beyond the system that tried to brand me as inferior. I had completed high school at the top of my class, even though I had to travel almost a hundred miles round trip every day (while passing the two white high schools along the way, one of which was literally within walking distance of Mama Ponk's house where I lived). Even in St. Louis, when working in dire circumstances in a downtown cafeteria, emboldened by the faith of my elders I found a way to move out of the pots-and-pans room and end up as a bank messenger. Though not the best job, this turned out to be a precursor to what was possible when I became a bank owner decades later in Tulsa. I had served our nation honorably in the United States Air Force and had gone on to college and professional post-graduate work. My life, like the lives of millions of African Americans, has been proof of what is possible in spite of the reality of the racial discrimination many of us faced. I knew who I was.

Yet internally, in this situation, I kept mulling in my head: Would those inside the big plantation house really know me? Would they be able to look beyond my color and welcome me to the supper table as one of them?

This is the dilemma that still haunts African Americans even as slavery and Jim Crow segregation recede further into the nation's past. Why? Perhaps it is because the issues of racism have never really been confronted, the healing conversation to bring understanding between whites and blacks has never really taken place. This is the conversation John Hope Franklin and others have tried to start. But as my own experience proves, the conversation is tantalizingly elusive.

As an African American, even as an educated professional well accepted by my white peers, I was well aware of the difficulty that could surround us in this setting. We all know the history of slavery and the long shadow of its aftermath. We all know about the struggles for equal participation, from Jackie Robinson to Marion Anderson. We know about the civil rights era and those who died and those who disappeared without a trace. We know about Selma and Montgomery and the dogs and the water hoses. We all know the music of that era, but I somehow felt that there would be no singing, no hand-holding and no closing of the eyes as we visualized a more perfect union and gave in to the power of song.

We shall overcome . . . we shall overcome.

We all may have embraced the notion that we had on some level overcome, but I knew that there would be no shared music tonight. Overcoming requires brave hearts and courageous souls. I felt that my presence, a lone black man in that setting, would evoke the reality of that transformative era, without any conversation. It would be much safer that way, but still uncomfortable.

Roselawn Plantation was not a modern college where we could talk harmoniously beyond the past and focus on the future. No, I had been invited to supper in the lap of the antebellum South. It would be difficult for me to sip wine out of a cut-glass goblet when surrounded by the remnants of an era that would have considered me chattel property. In all likelihood, I would be the only one whose ancestors had once been owned by other human beings. History will never erase that reality, and memory of its continuing impact will not be forgotten.

We had not yet parked the car, but I had already traveled hundreds of miles in my head. I remembered an evening when I had felt similarly alone in New York City, at once the home of Lady Liberty and yet a place where the lingering lessons of race and place manifested. I was invited to a literary reception on Fifth Avenue as a member of the Eudora Welty Advisory Board. As I left my hotel, I realized I had left the invitation on the bed. Without hesitation, I raced back to get the piece of paper that could vouch for me despite my color. Then, as I made my way along New York's busy streets, even with the invitation tucked inside my coat pocket, my mind focused on who would be present and the conversations that would unfold, and whether my small literary acclaim would be enough to balance out my race. I was thinking, *this is really not the place for me*, even though the purity of literature had secured my place.

The signs of "white only" and "colored" are gone, but they linger in many African Americans' minds. Unfortunately, such signs were a ubiquitous part of our landscape. Those were the signs that kept me and many African Americans out of the library and out of the public park. I learned as kid that I couldn't play with "them." Maybe I was afraid that the social protocol we expect would not work in such an environment and someone with just a bit too much wine would confront me.

"Why are you here? You can't play with us."

The line of racial division was so deep in the soil of the South when I was a child, a hard thunderstorm could not wash it away. There were just some things white people and black people didn't do together. We worked for them! We cleaned for them! We cooked for them! We tended to their children! We did not go to church together. We did not celebrate birthdays together. We sat in the backseats of their cars. We went to separate schools. We served the Champagne. We washed the goblets.

With such thoughts running through my head, how could I be excited over supper at Roselawn, and how could I be excited at seeing the plantation owner who represented much of what I wanted to forever forget? How would she respond to me when she was in her natural setting? Would the differences in our lives then and now be even more pronounced when we were surrounded by acres of cotton and, if Kathy and Mike were correct, incredible antiques? My carefully crafted resumé was dimming in the reality of what I was seeing and anticipating. I needed a level of self-confidence that seemed to have slipped away. Even being with Mike and Kathy was not making it any easier. Their confident sense of self was not transferable. Their presence was not enough to bolster my feelings. I needed my own confidence.

I appreciated Kathy and Mike for not rushing me right in. I was not ready to face what I felt awaited me—a house full of people who could have easily imagined themselves as occupants. And where would such an imagination leave me? I know Mike and Kathy were ready to get out of the hot car, stretch their legs, and breathe fresh air. It was all over their faces. And maybe my reluctance was all over mine. Unlike me, their places at the supper table had been secured long before they were born. They had the "pass" their color provided.

I suspected that the people inside Miss Camille's home would have no emotional racial issues to unravel. They could throw caution to the wind without having to deal with voices from their Poppa's front porch cautioning them to be careful. Mama Ponk would not be telling them to *just keep walking*. All my young life I was cautioned to be careful around white people, regardless of their social status. It was their color, somehow perceived by many to be divine. So much of my survival depended upon my understanding the limitations placed upon me because of my color. Being black was not a door-opener. Unfortunately, those lingering lessons of race and place were crowding around me. I tried to muster the fortitude needed to embrace myself just as I was—a black man, a descendant of slaves who had done well and made his people proud. I had little choice to do otherwise.

I had been invited to supper.

6

Uneasy Moments, Lingering Thoughts

"He had the uneasy manner of a man who is not among his own kind, and who has not seen enough of the world to feel that all people are in some sense his own kind." —Willa Cather

WE PARKED IN FRONT OF ROSELAWN AND KATHY TURNED OFF the engine. "Well, Clifton, this is where our little Camille grew up," she said matter-of-factly.

"It's certainly not the Southern farm and the small red-brick house I expected. You know, I haven't seen this much cotton growing since I was a child. It sure brings back memories."

"Well, I guess it would," Mike said, "but that was long ago."

Kathy spoke up, trying to take the edge off my obvious feelings. "You know, Clifton, much of this life is new to me. I'm not from the South and I'm white, so I can only imagine how you might be feeling. I can tell that you're anxious. But you'll do fine. The world has changed. We are all here together. We are all guests for supper."

"I know that. I just know that it took generations, as well as the civil rights movement, to secure my invitation."

"Don't let the look of this house and its history overwhelm you," Kathy added. "It can be very warm inside, I assure you. I've been here before."

I wanted to remind Kathy that her visit had been free of the stuffed paper bags, packed trunks, and overloaded suitcases of memories that served as lessons on how to be "colored." But I have always found it difficult to just come out and honestly say to a white person how it feels to be black. Maybe being a white Southerner himself and understanding himself the complexity of the divide is why former President Clinton had called on America to have a conversation about race. But even with the able help of the late black historian John Hope Franklin, a man I knew and admired greatly, the conversation ran into difficulty. Unfortunately, I can understand why. Nevertheless, I knew it remained a conversation that America needs to have.

Kathy had said to not let the house overwhelm me. She was too late. It already had. Not only had the mansion overwhelmed me, but I was adding to what was already weighing me down. My eyes fell upon what looked like doors to multiple small rooms under the steps. I immediately figured them to be quarters for the house servants—then and probably now. No thoughts of vintage wine were in my head. I was now trying to deal with how I would react and respond to the black servants. There was no need to point this out to Mike and Kathy. This concerned only me.

I wonder how many black servants are working today. I know the butler is going to open the door. What am I going to say to him?

Having come from a family of black servants, I knew the protocol. Back home, I would have gone to the back door, and the maid or butler would have come out, and I would say what I needed to say, or leave whatever I had been told to bring. If the servant who met me at the back door was an older female relative, I would be kissed on the forehead before departing through the back gate. Today, however, I would be a guest and as such I had to deal with protocol that I considered awkward at best. I could not live with myself if I did anything that hinted at ignoring the "help" or acting as if their humanity was not on a par with mine, as I had seen so many times before. Besides, I didn't want to create an awkward moment for my hostess and her other guests, whom I assumed would all be white.

I was relieved when Mike spoke up, voicing to some extent what I was bearing all by myself.

"Clifton, I can't begin to imagine how being here makes you feel. What you are dealing with is stuff I just never have to mess with."

"I know, Mike, that's the gift of your birth. Be grateful. Being black in a white Southern world required learning all the lessons—gentle lessons that taught us who and what to avoid, and harsh lessons in words, deeds, or clearly posted signs that reminded us of our place. I had no other choice than to learn them. It was complex and burdensome. I had to learn to live against my natural youthful inclinations. I had to be taught how to be colored."

"I never thought of you having to actually be taught how to live as a kid."

"Not just as a kid, but as a black kid. Double lessons to learn."

"Clifton, I know this is just me talking, but I think they'd want you to be right here today, sitting at the table with whomever and enjoying yourself. You deserve to be here."

He was right: I deserved to be at the table. In fact, my folks had deserved to be at the table two hundred or more years ago. All humanity has always deserved to be appreciated and celebrated. I knew I would go inside with them, but "deserved" to be there didn't hit me right, even though I understood what was being said. How does one earn the right to be human?

I kept thinking about the guests inside as I slowly and thoughtfully made my way out of the car. I knew we would be on the same plane professionally, but for me, they became the "white" kids back home who were already playing in the park—the park where I could never play, not even if it was empty. Now I could join them, without the need for protection and without a great-aunt to watch out for me.

I wasn't sure if I was ready to play.

There was no comforting song in my head, either. Church was over. James Gatson had locked the juke joint's doors. I followed Mike and Kathy up the tall steps that led up to the veranda. I felt heavy with a history that was uniquely my own as I laid my hands on the aged wooden stair rails, smooth and rounded from centuries of wear. Little Cliff was right beside me, reminding me of what could happen and what had happened in the past. At that moment, there was no bright conversation about a shared future.

All the while, my mind was working, not just about my place in the picture, but also about the small rooms under the steps. Who slept in them? I expected to see a black person emerge from under the steps at any minute, loaded down with laundry or trays of food. I was concerned that the servants would see me, dressed in a suit, not helping them with their work, but walking up the steps to go inside.

Of course, I know that society has undergone tremendous change since I was growing up. This is the twenty-first century, where even domestic work does not carry the stigma it once did. Domestic labor is often more reflective of choice, and in many cases it pays fair wages. However, this place where I was scheduled to be eating supper within the hour did not seem reflective of the twenty-first century. As we got to the top step, I braced myself to be met at the door by a black butler. A house this grand would automatically have a butler.

My mind was also troubled by a memory of missing an opportunity to live up to my own expectations of myself. Several years earlier, my wife, Barbara, and I had been guests of the Governor and First Lady of the State of Mississippi. My first book, *Once Upon a Time When We Were Colored,* had become very successful; hence the invitation to have breakfast with Governor and Mrs. Ray Mabus. On the morning of the breakfast, we were met at the front door by the mansion's butler. I will always remember him, tall, black, with chiseled features. In another world, he could have been a formidable African prince. In Mississippi, he was simply the butler. No handshakes and no personal greetings other than "good morning." He was on the job and we were anxious and nervous first-time guests.

Without fanfare he escorted us into the sitting room where the Old

South in ornate frames looked down from the walls as we waited. I felt as if their eyes were alive, watching our every move and finding it very difficult to understand our presence as guests and not as servants. When the gracious conversation and the Southern breakfast were over, he appeared as if by magic and escorted us out. I will never forget that I never asked his name. I didn't want this to happen with Miss Camille's butler. I was determined to do more than nod and say thank you.

We finally made it to the porch. I could hear the chatter and laughter inside and none of it was making me feel any better. I felt so close to the "park" and yet so far away. Such a feeling would be difficult to understand unless your life had been one where being left out and overlooked was customary. I had my ideas of what could be going on inside—white educators enjoying a life they had read about while the servants moved silently among them refreshing drinks and passing out small bites to eat. And I was about to be in the midst of them trying to find my place at the table.

I heard footsteps responding to Mike's knock on the door. I was still anxious. I tried to hide it and let some excitement show. Mike and Kathy looked excited, while I braced myself for the life behind the door. I could hear the knob being turned. I stood nervously as I waited to be ushered into history, as I had been in the Mississippi governor's mansion. When the door finally opened, instead of the chiseled face of a faithful black butler, it was Miss Camille, the lady whose handshake had held me captive several years earlier.

With the door now standing wide, she smiled at us and called back to the others. "Why, look, y'all, at who's here! It's Mike and Dr. Paget, and Mister Taulbert." Looking me directly in the eyes as if I had been expected for years, she said, "Mister Taulbert, I'm so glad to have you here with us. Now y'all come on in; we are all here. And we'll be getting ready for supper soon."

I was in the entryway before I knew it. Before I had a chance to respond to all the people introducing themselves and renewing friendships, I was introduced to the lone black female who was present. I did feel somewhat better now. We would both have to deal with the "colored" help. I learned that she was a South Carolina educator, someone Little Camille knew and invited to supper. I was glad she was there.

That's just like Camille to make sure that I was not alone.

Little Camille had proven herself to be a very thoughtful person, her deep Southern accent notwithstanding. Her thoughtfulness had left no indication of her privileged Southern upbringing. She had invited me to South Carolina to talk about community, but she also knew that we had to build it. This supper was just another informal way to build bridges, I suppose.

After introductions and pleasantries, Miss Camille took hold of my arm as if it was the most natural thing to do. She didn't ask. No permission was granted. It just happened. The years of absence made no difference. It was as if we had just talked the day before.

Despite this Southern mansion she called home and her thousands of acres of cotton land, I was slowly coming to the conclusion that she was definitely the same gracious older lady who had gently held my hand, when a quick handshake would have sufficed, on our first meeting. And she was the lady who had taken time to write me the gracious note. Both circumstances were contrary to what Little Cliff expected. My inner fears wanted to take me further back into my youth—with a conversation that only I could hear.

"Boy, who are you talking to out there?" Mama yelled from the back kitchen door.

At the time, more than fifty years ago, I was leaning into Aunt Mary Ann's wire mesh fence. Our houses were side by side, and Aunt Mary Ann was the housekeeper to our white doctor, Dr. Duke, and the nanny of sorts to his grandchildren. Oftentimes they would spend the night at her house.

"I'm playing with the white children at Auntie Mary's house," I yelled back to my mother. Even then, I already knew to describe them by color. I am sure they did likewise.

"You be careful. Make sure you don't hit one of them," Mother admonished from her kitchen door.

I heard her, but it didn't matter. We were having a good time, as any kids would do. However, when their parents came to pick them up, they drove away uptown, where the white people mostly lived, and I stayed behind in the world that was mine.

My memory may have been pulling me back to the reality of the past, but Miss Camille's hand on my arm was leading me forward. She walked me from the small hallway into the rest of the house, where I see what seemed to be all the Southern antiques and Victorian furniture that General Sherman had missed—velvet-covered couches and matching chairs, marble-topped tables with antique lamps lighting the high ceilings that never seemed to end. No doubt about it, I was in the Old South, and it looked as if the heavy drapes in the formal living room were determined to keep the twenty-first century at bay.

In the den, I took my seat alongside the others and joined in the conversation, managing to keep my internal thoughts to myself—that's one of the lessons I had learned. Except for Miss Camille, Little Camille, the Pagets, and several other locals including the black educator, all the other guests were from back east. I wondered about my fellow black guest. Was this her first time at Roselawn? How was she responding to the invitation and all the history that surrounded the home? Much of what we were seeing could have been in a museum.

While we guests all admired the trappings of elegance, I was well aware of the labor expended to ensure such a lifestyle, and I was well aware of the color of that labor. I sat quietly as someone held high and pretended to ring a cut-glass bell of the type that was once used to summon servants. I was trying to be at ease in a very uneasy situation. I prayed that the bell would be allowed to rest. I am sure that bell had no history for most of the guests, but its presence had many implications for me.

On the other hand, Miss Camille seemed determined to make me feel at home. I knew that at her age she had lived within the world of legal segregation and knew well what had to be instituted to keep it alive. She must have sensed how I was feeling, being in a home that was so closely associated with a past that neither of us created but that had nonetheless branded both of us. Miss Camille occasionally came over to where I was sitting and she always stopped to touch me on the arm before moving on.

After I allowed myself to relax a bit into the situation and the small talk, I realized that I still needed to use the restroom. Badly. The cascading memories from my childhood had blocked my need. But now that I had settled in, the urge was back.

Bathrooms were a significant dividing line in the South when I was growing up, and it amazes and upsets me that I am still impacted by what I learned as a child. I'd just as soon pretend not to have to use the restroom in certain settings. I am certain that this was not an issue for the white people who were gathered in Miss Camille's den. I'm sure they felt free to answer a call from nature. But in the bad old days, even nature had to abide by the rules of segregation. I would not have been allowed to even think of using the same restroom as whites. When in their presence and nature called, we knew not to answer. Little Cliff's voice in my head was as clear as yesterday reminding me.

As badly as I needed to relieve myself, I was determined to "hold it." With all of us laughing and talking, I'm sure that none of the others was aware of my consternation. I was dressed right. I had accolades. I had traveled. I almost looked the part, except for the voice in my head.

Little Cliff's voice had me back home in Glen Allan where as a young boy I experienced my first and only face-to-face conversation about the use of an indoor "white only" toilet. This early harsh lesson in race and place has not been forgotten.

My whole family as well as our friends were delighted that I had moved from the cotton fields and gotten the inside job at the Hilton Food Store, especially as it was usually reserved for white boys. I still recall the first day of work and how well it started out. Mr. Hilton, the owner, walked me through the storeroom where the boxes of canned food and dry foodstuffs were stored, waiting to be put out on shelves. Everything was explained in explicit detail. Nothing was left to chance. After that part of the tour, we went into the main store where customers, mostly white farmers, many of whom Mr. Hilton knew personally, were milling around. I stood off to the side and watched as Mr. Hilton talked to the white customers and occasionally nodded to the black customers as they came in and went about their shopping. I just stood back, watching it all and waiting his turn with me. Finally, his greetings were over and together we made our way to the back of the store where the big white porcelain and stainless steel meat locker and counter were located. I was shown how to store the meat and told that I'd eventually be taught to cut up chickens and pork loins. This was going to be a real job. I was excited.

Then, while standing behind the sparkling white meat case, Mr. Hilton, tall and slightly balding with a ruddy complexion, looked down at his shoes and then up at the ceiling fan, as if he was thinking of how to craft his next words. I just stood there. He was white and I knew to just wait on his next move. Another lesson on how to cut meat or treat the customers was forthcoming, I was sure. That would not be the case. Instead of the instructions I expected, he looked at me as if I had done something terribly wrong. I didn't know what to do. I had not waited on a customer. I had not cut up a precious pork loin the wrong way. I could not imagine what I had done in less than fifteen minutes. I just stood there, speechless. In the world of my youth, you didn't ask questions of adults, and especially of white people. I watched his face change from the informing boss to a Southern white man, the face we had been taught to fear, respect and, if at all possible, stay clear of. I watched as his eyes narrowed and his lips started to tremble. With his shaking white finger close to my young black face, he pointed with his other hand to a small closed door in front of us. I had no idea what was behind the door. It was my first time ever behind the meat counter of his store. The words from his mouth startled me, but they were perfectly clear. I was clearly reminded of who I was to him, as if I had come there without that knowledge.

"That's *our* toilet over there!"

I knew from my elders not to say one word. So I stood motionless and took all that he was saying.

"Under no circumstances are you to ever go inside."

Still, I just stood there. What else could I have done? He was white in Mississippi and I needed the job. I still find his next response rather strange.

"Don't ask me why."

Mr. Hilton must have known that asking "why" would be the next natural inquiry. I am sure he would have asked. But I wasn't him. I was black. He was white. So I just stood there.

"Just don't ever use it. Is this clear?"

His entire face had turned red and his lips had quivered and his hands had quivered.

I never would have asked why. Part of learning how to be "colored" was the lesson of not ever questioning white people. Later that day, as I passed Mr. Gatson's juke joint on my walk home, I would be comforted to hear Fats Domino's New Orleans-inflected voice making its way out of the joint and across a ditch that separated us. "Ain't That a Shame" would became the theme of that day in my life.

No explanation was given. I didn't expect one. My natural needs had no bearing on him. I knew that I'd have to use the toilet, but to use that the indoor one would mean being fired or even worse. Then I saw him walk over to the back door and look out and then look back at me. His look said it all. At the back of the store, there was a wooded, snake-infested area that bordered Lake Washington. Without anything else being said, I knew my place.

That day in Mr. Hilton's store, there were no wise elders by my side to temper the tone of his words, and I never told my folks about this incident. Somehow I knew they had their own humiliating incidents, and they had just sucked it up and moved on. And now I had been initiated into the world of "them and us" that my folks had faced all their lives.

Yes, times changed, but I was still black and very well aware of the years of struggle just to gain access to a public toilet in South Carolina, not to mention a private john in a Southern mansion.

However, while I had inwardly determined to "hold it," out of the clear blue, Miss Camille appeared from the kitchen and made her way across the room. When she had made her way to where I was sitting, she leaned into my ear and said quietly, "Mister Taulbert, if you need to use the facilities, it's just around the corner. You can go through the parlor and turn right. It will be on your left."

Before I could thank her, she had walked off, leaving me with her permission to respond to nature as any other human would. I knew I was not in Glen Allan, and she was definitely not Mr. Hilton. Her directness surprised me, but she seemed not to have noticed my surprise. Maybe, she remembered that we had come from the same Southern world. She knew the world that was once called "colored" and all it meant for the both of us.

I simply excused myself from the group and headed out to find the guest bathroom—for me a journey into the world that had once excluded me. On my way, I passed by open doors where I casually glanced in at some of the most beautiful antique beds and accompanying pieces of period furniture I had ever seen.

I had been taken by surprise. Miss Camille had known exactly the right thing to do and say, and it was not what Little Cliff would have expected from someone of her age and position.

When I returned to the den, I learned that supper was almost ready. I assumed that while I was in the bathroom, one of the servants had come from the back and informed them. I was still on alert as to how I would respond to the black servants. I figured they would be showing up any minute as everyone was standing up and making their way to the exquisitely set table, which was as long and as elegant as the one my wife and I shared with the Governor of Mississippi and his wife. That table looked wonderful. Great Southern food was generously laid out, as were graceful, cut-crystal wine glasses. Miss Camille offered grace and invited us to start. The feast began.

As I think about that unexpected evening inside Miss Camille's home, and how at home and uneasy I felt at the same time, I understand that the bridge to close the racial divide is one we must build together. For many, the reach across the divide may not be easy—lingering history is powerful and not easily overcome. For some, it can be an invitation to supper.

The meal was wonderful, and so was the conversation. I was really surprised that not one black servant ever showed up. *Maybe they are off for the weekend. But then who announced that supper was ready?*

Freed from anxiety about the servants, I focused on the conversations, which were all about education. It was as if while I was using the restroom everyone else had come to an agreement that there would be no talk about the Civil War, slavery, or race. I was relieved, yet disappointed. This was a gathering of people I could have invited into the world that I lived with on an almost daily basis. Would I have done so? I don't know. The opportunity never came. Our particular Southern history is just not an easy subject to discuss, even though reasons to do so are all around us. Perhaps if we had we all could have left the mansion one step closer to what is required to remodel the nation.

When our meal was finally over, Miss Camille invited us back to the den. Then, as we made ready to leave for the evening, we gathered our belongings and waited for our housing assignments. For me, this was always one of those moments when I'd keep my fingers crossed; I paid close attention to where I would be assigned to sleep. I was not yet ready to throw caution to the wind, and neither was Little Cliff who stood close by my side, listening.

As we left, Miss Camille pulled me aside and quietly said she would be attending my lecture the next day. This was totally unexpected. She was not an educator—I knew that now. She had nothing to do with professional development for South Carolina educators. Why would a wealthy white planter want to sit in an uncomfortable college classroom to hear me talk? I did thank her, though, said goodbye, and then made my way down the steep steps to the car, but not before casting a glance at the doors to the small rooms under the steps.

By now, it was pitch dark, but still humid, and as the lights came on from the various cars, the mansion loomed even bigger and even more of a relic from the past. With Miss Camille and her dog watching from the veranda, Kathy and Mike and I waved as we piled into the car. My experience had not been what I expected. I never saw the black servants and heard no conversation about their whereabouts. *They must be off for the weekend,* I thought again as we drove off into the dark night.

7

Bearing Witness to the Possibilities

"It's a journalist's job to be a witness to history. We're not there to worry about ourselves. We're there to try and get as near as we can, in an imperfect world, to the truth and get the truth out."
—*Robert Fisk*

LEAVING ROSELAWN THAT NIGHT WAS LIKE SLIPPING AWAY from my past under the cover of darkness in hopes that it was left behind. No conversation emerged with my friends in the rental car around plantation life and its haunting impact upon my life. We talked about the food and the vintage wine and about Miss Camille. Soon we arrived at our assigned B&B, a somewhat small and sterile modern version of a Southern plantation home, definitely not a Roselawn or a Melrose; still, as I made my way up the stairs to my room, I wondered if I might be the first person of color to sleep there. But I was too emotionally exhausted to think further. I just cleaned up and went to bed, history and all.

Southern mornings come soon. Before I knew it, the morning sun was shining in my face. It wouldn't do to oversleep and let anybody say that "the black guy" was the reason we were late getting to the college. I quickly got ready and ran downstairs, only to be relieved that I was the first person up. Before long the back veranda was abuzz with breakfast chatter as the others straggled down. After biscuits, eggs, homemade jelly and hot coffee—I never liked coffee—we confronted the already rising humidity and heat and made our way back to the car, piling in like we were back in college, not professional adults on our way to teach. For a brief moment, I felt as if we were all one.

My mind, though, was already wandering back to last night's whispered conversation when Miss Camille told me that she would be a guest at my lecture. I tried to imagine her in my classroom. I couldn't. I was pretty sure that she would be the only person present who owned a plantation reaching back to antebellum history and listed in the National Register. Little Cliff was still apprehensive. I knew that I would be basing my talk on the people from the segregated community of my childhood—a world that had been created by people like Miss Camille for their benefit. I could not alter my talk. The handouts had already been made.

I didn't know all that much about Allendale County, but I knew that it was culturally akin to Glen Allan, which meant that the racial divide was deep and accepted as a way of life, even though integration had brought about much change. Despite our festive last evening at Roselawn—with its revelations for Little Cliff—I was well aware that the social implications of legal segregation lingered in way too many parts of our country. We had all learned the lessons of the "color." I had run into that reality in so many places, North and South, and, even more unfortunately, in our schools where the next generation should be taught their responsibilities to each other.

This would be part of my conversation today, the importance of building community to create and sustain a just society. Teaching from this perspective was challenging and even more so in many of our Southern schools where the lessons of race and place still impacted our thinking and our actions. In too many of our rural and Southern schools, this reality was still reflected in the test scores of many of our youth, especially those who looked like me. In some places, the lack of community was so evident that a whole pedagogy has grown up around how to teach the black child in our integrated setting. So, in my sessions, I would address the need for adult educators to create a school culture that was welcoming for all, one where high expectations existed for every student. To do so, I would take them back to my examples of Glen Allan and the challenges I faced while growing up during segregation. If Miss Camille came, she would be hearing the other side of an era she knew well, my recollection of how a few determined black people built an environment to stave off the impact of racism. I wasn't sure I wanted her to come. Even though she was confounding Little Cliff's expectations at every turn, I was still not quite sure who this lady was.

Needless to say, we arrived at the campus and swam through the humidity into the building; how I thanked God for air conditioning! Some of the South Carolina educators were already gathered and were chattering in groups of twos and threes, but mostly among their own race. I suspected this would be the case. I knew the difficulty in living beyond that social divide, even in the twenty-first century. I thought back to last night and how Miss Camille, of all people, had rescued me from my intense need to use the bathroom. That was an intentional act on her part—the same type of intentionality that would be required of all our educators if they were to create an embracing and welcoming culture and community for all students.

As I set up for the lecture, I knew I had work to do to create community between myself and the educators and to give them another picture of how both races can interact together for the benefit of the youth under their watch. I realized that I had to be intentional about moving beyond my personal ghosts. I could not let my past prevent me from reaching forward to the future. I had to embrace and promote the experiences of brotherhood and sisterhood that I had experienced. Just as I had deserved a higher vision while a student in Glen Allan, those young people being taught by these South Carolina Low Country educators deserved to see possibilities for their shared future. They needed to see new models lived out in their presence that were respectful of all. My work was cut out for me, and I knew it. I didn't need the complication of hosting a wealthy white plantation owner.

I began to worry about Miss Camille's potential impact upon my presen-, tation. Would I be overly solicitous? Would I water down my conversation? I could not afford to reinforce the very thing I was trying to change. We had to move beyond the legacy of separate-but-equal. I didn't want Miss Camille's presence to minimize getting this message across. I could feel a headache heading my way. I finally concluded it would be best if she stayed put in the mansion this morning.

I QUICKLY GOT EVERYTHING set and then stood at the door to welcome the teachers. As I watched the room fill up, I was interrupted by Little Camille, who was facilitating the academy. She stuck her head in the door and with her warm Southern voice welcomed me to the college. All the arrangements had been her doing.

"Clifton, did you rest well last night? I sure hope so," Camille called out to me, her arms stuffed with papers and books. "Did you get breakfast?" Without giving me a chance to answer, she continued. "We've got juice and sweet things in the conference room through that door right down the hall to your right—and the men's room is also right down the hall."

Knowing that Camille could talk faster than I could, I answered quickly. "We had a great breakfast. Can I do anything to help you out?"

"No, just make sure you have everything you need in your room. Everybody is so excited to hear you."

Little Camille was a marvel. She was of this land, and yet she saw possibilities for a future that was so different from the world that surrounded her. She had yet to surprise me by doing something contrary to the respect for each other that I believed important for all to embrace. I shook my head as I watched her scurry off to take care of someone else. She had not changed from the lady I had met years earlier in the lobby of the Philadelphia Hotel. She was really good at taking care of all of us.

By now my room was full. Everybody was seated and I was ready for the opening conversation. Suddenly, I could hear Little Camille's unmistakable Southern voice headed my way. She literally buzzed around the corner, her face and eyes filled with excitement.

"Clifton, I can't believe it, but Mama is here."

I gulped! I had convinced myself that Miss Camille would not show up.

By now, voices from Glen Allan refused to be left out of the conversation. While I was trying to make ready to talk and to welcome Miss Camille, my mind was back home remembering when it was absolutely necessary to have a white person validate what you were doing. I saw it all the time, at our schools and in our community—the white community leader dropping by to indicate everything was in order, so to speak. Our efforts had to have their seal of approval. Was that why Miss Camille was coming? After all, she was from that era.

Fortunately, Little Camille had no idea of the running commentary in my head. And I have no idea if she had one of her own running. Both races had learned not to talk about things that really mattered. Sharing our feelings honestly is part of the conversation on race we have not had the courage to have.

So Miss Camille was no longer a potential visitor. I now had an object lesson on community building just outside the building. I encourage educators and business people to step outside their comfort zones, to embrace the new opportunities that come their way. I encourage them not to be socially strangled by the past. I encourage them in no uncertain terms to make room at their table for all. To drive my point home, I sometimes tell the story of the Jewish lady in Glen Allan who, after allowing us to pick up pecans in her uptown orchard, invited my cousin and me into her home for a salami sandwich, angel food cake, and my first cup of matzo ball soup. Miss Freid invited us into her life, which was not customary. I was apprehensive. It was outside my comfort zone and the rules of segregation. As much as I wanted to say, "No, thank you," we accepted her invitation, which must have been difficult for her to offer. We were not admonished for tracking mud into her den, and we eventually found ourselves in her kitchen. I must admit that at first it was uncomfortable, but she went out of her way to ease our anxiety. The food was good. Mrs. Freid stretched her table to include us. Now I had to buck up and do likewise. Miss Camille's presence would be the lesson I had to live out, rather than talk about or be nervous over.

She was bringing a lot of history with her, and so was I.

Although her daughter didn't say to go meet her, I went to the window and looked out at the long black Cadillac parked along the curb. I could see Miss Camille, as well-dressed as when I first saw her, slowly walking in her three-inch heels toward the front door of the college. Without thinking more, I excused myself to the class and went to greet her.

I got there just in time to help her save some of her strength for another day. Our gazes met as I became the Southern gentleman holding the big, heavy door to the lobby. Her eyes were smiling like any mom's or grandmother's would. At her age, had she been black, I would have leaned down and given her a hug and maybe a kiss on her powdered cheek. But she wasn't a black grandmother or an older black aunt. She was a white Southern plantation owner. That was her reality, and the lingering history that stood at the door with me was my mine.

Instead, without warning and quite naturally, with all the people in the lobby looking on, she gave me the warm hug and the peck on the cheek. Without fanfare, she slipped her arm in mine as if it were the most natural thing in the world to do, and we walked to the classroom where earlier I had privately hoped that she would not show up.

In those few seconds, I pushed my apprehensions aside. The chasm that divided our lives was not as wide as I had thought. We could reach out to each other and it was our choice to do so. I have no idea what was going through her head in driving to the college to once again hear this black Southerner talk. I just know that without planning it, Miss Camille became part of my lesson plan as she put her arm in mine. After all, that's what community building is all about, trusting others, trusting those who may be different from one's self. Together, our walk was one of trust and respect, a walk I could not have made as a child, and no doubt one that many from her generation would have viewed as socially unacceptable.

I didn't have to say a word to my class about what was taking place or how I viewed it. They saw what could be possible. They were observing it all—race, gender, social standing, and generations together. For the educators that morning, that was what the young Americans they were teaching needed to see on a daily basis. If we are to lay to rest the lessons of race and place, our actions must propel us all to intentionally and consistently move beyond our comfort zones, as we were doing even in historic Allendale, South Carolina, on a hot summer's day.

If only the teachers had known all that was going through my mind, they would have had an even greater appreciation of that morning and for any outward calmness I possessed. Miss Camille and I were walking out from a shadow that surely followed both lives. I will never know the conversation that ensued in Miss Camille's head the first time she heard me speak or when I was a first time guest at her historic mansion. She, like me, never let on.

Now I had to make sure that I stayed on track. Though sidetracked by my very real past, I understood that I had to challenge all those present to rise to a higher level of teaching and to lay aside any social and cultural holdovers from our once legally segregated world.

I glanced at the few black educators in my group. There was little doubt that we were not in the Allendale of the 1950s. Change had come. However, the black teachers, like me, were well aware of the social divide that still existed in the county. I had much work to do as I talked to the present about the future, and as I reprimanded the past—much of which would have been embodied in the presence of Miss Camille, who was to me a living icon of the "Old South."

Over the years, I have fully embraced the critical role of leadership in setting the social tone of any organization. As Peter Senge said in *The Fifth Discipline*, "We must challenge our mental models." That day I had to challenge mine as I would be challenging my participants, who now included Little Camille's mother, to challenge theirs. To challenge our familiar ways of doing things is the prerequisite for building and sustaining good community where we live and work, especially in classrooms where we teach. And for our children, what they observe of us will help set them on their course of social action or no action.

I STILL HAD TO get Miss Camille seated. In our small colored school in Glen Allan, Miss O'Bannon, our white superintendent, always sat up front when visiting, as would any other white person. But on this day in Allendale, as we entered the classroom, Miss Camille whispered in my ear, "Clifton, find me a seat in the back, if you please."

Has she been this way all her life?

I peered over the crowd, looking for a seat on the back row. All the while, the teachers were watching. They knew historical social protocol was being broken. Not only did she take her seat among the others, she also took out her note pad. Miss Camille had come prepared to hear my lecture and to take notes. I watched as those sitting around her did likewise. How I wished that such a picture could have been Southerners' shared reality in the past when our worlds were separate with little or no thought toward equality. I saw so much in that very simple setting of diverse educators and one unexpected guest. Had such social civility existed between the races, the bloody days of Selma would never have been, and I expect that America would have been on an entirely different path socially, economically and even politically.

With Miss Camille seated, I began our journey back to my Mississippi Delta and into the unselfish and influential lives of my elders—ordinary, everyday African Americans—the core of my workshop conversation. Using my own life as an example, I wanted the class to see what was possible then and what is even more possible now. I wanted them to recognize and embrace the power of their influence, regardless of their race, social status, or the race or social status of the children they were teaching. I knew all of this to be of real importance for both the white and black educators who in that South Carolina county would be teaching mostly African American students from economic backgrounds not too different from mine as a child. I wanted them to understand the importance of teaching and planning with high expectations for each child. My elders had left me with the notion that, even though I couldn't play in the park or use the library, I could still dream and work to have the future I wanted.

I unashamedly shared the struggle of my own life: born to a teenage mother, cared for by various relatives, and yet, because of the community built around me, all those "porch people" stepping up, I was able to survive and thrive. I considered my life proof of the power of community as I talked about the unselfishness I encountered and how it protected my dreams from the harsh realities of legal segregation. I could see Miss Camille feverishly writing notes, which I could have understood had she been the retired teacher I first took her for.

In my talk, I told the truth as I understood and had witnessed it. It was important to do so. My listeners were all Southerners, and I am sure, like me, had their own private truths. But too often, those were the conversations left unshared. Now, as these white and black educators were teaching side by side, it became even more important to break down those longstanding cultural barriers so that the youth they were teaching would be receiving their very best.

The morning workshop evoked so much participation that without Little Camille standing at the back and pointing at her watch, I might have forgotten the break. During the break, I went back to chat with her mother.

"Clifton, this is all so good. I am just amazed at how you can take us back to your childhood and make us all wish it to have been our own." And then, thoughtfully and quietly, she added, "I know of those times."

Certainly we both knew. How could we not? She had to know the inhumanity of the system of segregation. She had to have seen it up close, but back in her times, as it was with me in my time, it was simply how things were. It was all well-orchestrated to keep us in a place defined by others, where some were valued and others not valued except as a ready labor supply. These unfortunate actions were in place for hundreds of years, and the thinking that evolved survived the Civil War and set the stage for the Jim Crow laws which were in place when I was growing up.

For the majority of those who looked like me, success would not be theirs. Truth be told, we could have all failed. Unlike other ethnic groups who immigrated through Ellis Island and similar ports of entry, we were unable to change our names to better assimilate. Our color traveled with us and still today dictates much about us. This reality still shows up in some of our educational institutions, and so there is still the need to change hearts and minds.

This is what I hope to accomplish as I travel and lecture. This is why Little Camille had invited me to South Carolina, to share the timelessness and universality of the power of community to change lives. I want to inspire others to create a culture of high expectations not unlike the culture I experienced in Glen Allan—a culture that intentionally went against the odds. Many of the places where we would lecture in South Carolina were reminiscent of Glen Allan with its abundance of poor African Americans. Camille knew I could have failed to escape the box that segregation had prepared for me. I didn't fail. She wanted the teachers to know what was possible, no matter how dire the circumstances might look. She wanted them to know my book, *Eight Habits of the Heart,* which outlined the unselfish actions of the people who rallied to my rescue.

That was my morning lecture. I dissected all eight habits—*Nurturing*

Attitude, Responsibility, Dependability, Friendship, Brotherhood & Sisterhood, High Expectations, Courage and Hope and personalized each as we discussed them. Miss Camille was quietly taking notes throughout.

For me, survival with a future would not have happened had not my elders unselfishly built community. But I have yet to be able to fully put into words my deep impressions of how I felt when I was surrounded by them. No number of words can honestly convey those feelings.

I captured the generosity of their hearts as best as I could in my writings, but I always wanted to say so much more. I had feelings that I could not put in words. In some way, I understand when Miss Camille replied with just five words about a history about which volumes have been written. "Yes, I know. I know." She told me this while holding onto my hand. At that moment, I wanted to know what she knew. I wanted to know how she had been raised and how she felt about the intentional separation of the races. My life and hers had been shaped by that historical Southern way of living. I had never had the opportunity to talk up close and personal with someone like her. She was a perfect person to give a firsthand account of the other side of the story. She had the race, the age, the position in society, and the legacy of her prominent Southern family. I knew the lessons of race and place had followed my life. But what had followed her life and the lives of her peers?

No more words were forthcoming. However, her eyes, the pat on the back of the hand, and the tone of her voice carried feelings that I would be left to interpret on my own. Words are necessary, but deep impressions matter most and sometimes cannot be expressed in words, especially in complicated situations. Maybe, just maybe, for me that day, true emotions were being expressed and mere words would have simply gotten in the way. I may never know the depth of her feelings or the particulars we all would like to know, but I was there when the five words were uttered. Only she knew where she was coming from that day, but her actions spoke most eloquently.

AFTER THE FIRST BREAK, my lesson plan called for more of the same, but I needed to put in a bit more energy, to keep pushing the participants beyond their comfort zones. I wanted these teachers to really embrace the transformative possibilities embedded in the process of building community, living out the eight habits of the heart on a daily basis in the schools where they taught and on the playgrounds where the children played.

At the end of the second break, at noon, Miss Camille made ready to leave. I watched as she carefully put her notes away. She had enjoyed herself. I could tell as she took the time to throw a pretend kiss to all the teachers. I watched as they all responded with pretend catches. Yes, she was more than an ordinary guest. By now, they knew she was Mrs. Camille Cunningham Sharp of Roselawn Plantation, and I was still flustered as to why she'd spent her morning with us. She said she had come to hear me. But why me? Our paths had only crossed once before. I was not her son's best friend. I was not the successful son or grandson of a bridge partner she had known all her life or the son of a family she had grown up with. I was simply the black kid from Glen Allan who had somehow managed to survive in a segregated world that she had no doubt watched safely from her parlor's front window.

Much of that world was now gone, but its social implications remain strong—the vestiges and residue of the past. Years ago it would have taken courage for such a noteworthy citizen to come to a lecture given by a black man, to publicly lean on his arm, and to sit in the back row among ordinary people. To go against the prevailing social winds of her day would have required unprecedented courage at a time when it looked as if that way of life would continue forever. However, to come on the day she did, when it wasn't required or when no one was there to take notice, simply required a will of her own and maybe reasons I'll never know. I watched as she gracefully made her way to the lobby of the college where she said goodbye to some others who were milling around, including her daughter.

I heard Camille calling out to me.

"Mister Taulbert, Mama's ready to go. Want me to walk her to the car?"

I blurted out, "No, I'll walk her to the car."

Miss Camille simply smiled, as any mother or grandmother would do when a man of whatever age volunteers to walk her to the car. As earlier that morning, she slipped her arm in mine and we headed to the door and to the heat and humidity.

"It's awfully hot out there. Let me get my keys out."

She rummaged around in her purse and finally came up with her key chain. As we walked outside, I think steam was rising from the earth. It didn't help matters that her Cadillac was black and absorbed heat.

I stood with her as she unlocked the car door and held it open to let out the stifling, trapped hot air. We talked while she allowed the heat to escape.

"Mister Taulbert, you think you'll be back next year?"

"I am not sure—these consulting contracts are not guaranteed. I just have to wait and see. If invited, though, I'll be back." I was waiting for her to say more. Instead she just smiled. Her morning was over and she was returning to Roselawn. She had a cotton plantation to run. She mentioned that she had to stop off and pick up some mechanical parts to take back to "the boys," as she called her workers, who also included her only son, Don, as well as his son, the blond-haired young Carl, the apple of Miss Camille's eye.

I waited until she got situated in the car with the engine and air roaring. Through the open window, she gave another pat on the back of my hand as it rested on the door I had just closed for her. Somewhere along our journey, a new future was being crafted from a past that had once imprisoned both of us. I could sense it, even though I was still somewhat cautious. I have found that the impact of being taught how to be "colored" is not so easily ignored. Our paths crossing and our ongoing conversations still felt somewhat surreal. With the voice of Little Cliff steadfast, I found myself, after the fact, questioning the depth or genuineness of the emotions that seemed to be surfacing for both of us. Our shared humanity seemed to have trumped all that we knew to be the acceptable Southern protocol. That whole morning was flying in the face of its history. I knew this, but I was still trying to understand it.

When I returned to the building, I observed some of the black and white educators now mingling in the lobby, not quite as separated by race as they had been at the start of the day. Maybe the lessons on building community as personal action were catching hold. Certainly, they had been part of an unplanned and unrehearsed show-and-tell. They had seen Miss Camille, a Southern icon, reach beyond what might have been comfortable at earlier points along her journey. Hopefully, they bore witness to the offer of my arm as I pushed against the voices in my head, and her gracious acceptance of it.

That afternoon I never mentioned Miss Camille's unexpected visit and what I thought it may have signified. I probably should have, but I kept those thoughts to myself and trusted that people had observed and learned what they needed.

8

Bearing the Burden of History

"None knows the weight of another's burden." —George Herbert

AT THE END OF THE WEEK, I RETURNED HOME TO TULSA WITH my head filled with more questions than answers, as my past collided with my present. While I should have been focusing on the words from our evaluator, Dr. Paget, I could not stop thinking about the invitation to Miss Camille's home and how surprised I had been upon discovering her real identity. I tried to share this with my wife and a few others, but again, words were not sufficient to describe an emotional journey I barely understood myself. Miss Camille's graciousness, they comprehended. After all, we are in the twenty-first century. But I was experiencing all of this through eyes from a different place and time in history. I soon began to realize that the difficulty I had in explaining may have been because this was my personal journey, one that dealt with the world I had known and the one I was working to see. In any case, I knew that my encounter with Mrs. Camille Cunningham Sharp was turning out to be like none other.

Miss Camille was not the first white Southerner to shake my hand or listen to my lecture. I knew the great Southern writer Eudora Welty. I remember our first face-to-face meeting. I was a guest in her Jackson, Mississippi, home (now a museum). My first book, *Once Upon a Time When We Were Colored*, was on her living room coffee table right in the midst of all her other books. I even had a cold Coca-Cola at her house, straight from the original-style glass bottle. We rode together to her alma mater, Mississippi College for Women, where we were both speakers. She was from the same era as Miss Camille, but her presence did not evoke the same feelings. In the presence of Miss Welty, I did not feel intimidated—in awe, yes, but not intimidated.

But I was in the presence of Miss Camille, childhood memories flooded through me in ways I had never experienced. The drama in my head was being played out as if it was still the 1950s and I had become a little "colored" boy once again in Glen Allan, where I knew my place in society and her place as well.

As I reflected on that, my head welcomed the voice of the great-great grandpa I had never known. All my life I had heard about Grandpa Sid and his love for the hymn "Precious Lord." He was Great-aunt Elna's daddy, and in hard times I would hear her humming and singing, every now and then, *Precious Lord, take my hand, lead me on, let me stand.* Their song became mine as I tried to make sense of this new journey. I did need someone bigger than me as a guide. After all, such graciousness from someone like Miss Camille was not commonplace in my life. Even with her acts of kindness in my head, I was reminded to be cautious. After all, she was a white plantation owner—one who was still growing thousands of acres of cotton. Was it insensitive to invite me, the descendant of slaves, to her home? She knew I would see the fields. Or, was something bigger at work?

Had she become a door that was leading me down an unfamiliar path, one apparently I had to travel? Had I become a door for her to travel a path she needed as well? I wanted to know why she had been drawn to me and my stories, laced as they were with the reality of what it was like to live in the shadow of the "Big House." I wanted to know why she found it so easy to slip her arm in mine or to interrupt her daily routine to come and hear me speak.

MY LIFE CONTINUED ALONG its own routine, which kept South Carolina on my mind. We worked out an agreeable contract, and I was looking forward to returning for the next summer's workshops. I had hoped to be invited back. I wanted to hold that very important conversation with Miss Camille about the impact her presence had upon me. I wanted to get her personal thoughts on the civil rights movement. I had questions—some of my own and some crafted from conversations with family and friends—to which I thought she could provide answers.

I had yet to fully understand the motivation behind her unexpected and unexplained graciousness toward me. Is it possible that, at that season of her life, Miss Camille was placing her shoulders underneath the burden of our shared past? Did she intend that ordinary acts from her heart would become a new reality in my heart? Maybe if I were to see her again, I would have an opportunity to observe closely and ask every question I could not answer. I even found myself practicing questions to ask her. I just wanted her five-word commentary to be expanded, hopefully helping me to better understand the burdens that became mine.

Yes, I bear burdens, those I knew about and those that were brought to light in Alex Haley's historic family saga, *Roots*. From Kunta Kinte, I learned more of my history than I had known before. *Roots* also left an indelible imprint in my heart of how we were perceived as slave labor and nothing more. Along with so many others, I still bear the emotional scars from a wound that has never properly healed. When we thought it was over, with an Emancipation Proclamation on our side, it appeared again in the "black codes." And then Jim Crow and legal segregation began to weave their way into the very fabric of our nation. This was the way of life I knew as a child and the only way of life my elders had ever known.

My legally segregated past is intertwined in the fabric of my life. Little Cliff knows this and stays in a protective mode, always cautioning me to be careful, which is why I found it difficult to accept Miss Camille's graciousness at face value. Now, with my renewed invitation in hand, I was headed back to South Carolina. Maybe this time I would leave with answers that made sense to me and to others.

I was also pleased to continue my conversation about building community. I knew that people could cross the racial divide and embrace our shared humanity. I had first seen it in the military. The Air Force interrupted segregation for airmen during the 1960s. I can vividly recall the ritual of relieving all of us young soldiers of our former lives and even our former looks. By the time the military finished with us, we had no hair and were all similarly dressed in ill-fitting clothes. Despite the cultures we brought from home and despite our lessons of race and place, the military was committed to creating an environment of inclusivity as it formed us into a unit. This is what building community could do. Now I could hardly wait to get back to South Carolina. I felt as if I had two missions to accomplish.

By now, too, I was sensing that my invitation to South Carolina was no accident. Without that initial near-miss invitation that was extended in the lobby of the Wyndham Hotel in Philadelphia, my path would never have crossed that of Miss Camille.

THE DAY TO RETURN finally came. This time, I was being met at the airport in Savannah, Georgia, by Frances Chavous, another white Southern lady and one of Little Camille's childhood friends. I had already met Frances on one of my earlier visits to Allendale; we shared a fondness for NPR and books. So I looked forward to our ride to Allendale. During the drive, I learned from Frances that Miss Camille had agreed to host us again at Roselawn.

This time, I was excited; not jumping up and down, but excited. I now had a mission to accomplish. Who had I become to Miss Camille? And who had Miss Camille become to me? Roselawn, though the very real picture of the Old South, was emotionally intimidating, but I was determined not to be taken back to a world of servitude. And Miss Camille? Well, she had somehow found my arm to lean on. It would be good to see her again, even though I anticipated conflicting moments. I wanted a more in-depth conversation about race and place from her perspective. I wanted more than just my assumptions, no matter how real I felt them to be.

"Great news," I quickly answered. As Frances whisked us through the Southern countryside, it would have been a perfect time for me to find out more about Miss Camille and the history of Roselawn Plantation and maybe even ask about how local people had handled the civil rights movement. Frances would have been the perfect person to ask. She and Little Camille had grown up together. But again I missed an opportunity to ask the questions that really mattered. Slavery and all its offshoots are still difficult topics to raise in racially mixed company. Instead of being a brave writer, I privately flashed back to the plantation and to those small rooms I had observed beneath the steep steps. These were servants' quarters, but I had yet to see servants.

I'll see the black servants this time. This is a weekday and not a weekend, so I feel sure that I'll meet them. I bet Frances knows who they are.

It would be important to me to honor and respect the servants' humanity and not pass by them as if they weren't even present. Being the overlooked "help" was often discussed in black homes. My mother was "help" and her conversations are not forgotten. I wanted Miss Camille's black help to know my name and just as I wanted to know their names. I felt that if I could get to know them, I would also get a clearer picture of who this lady really was, now that her actions toward me, the visiting writer, were turning out to be much different than expected.

As Frances and I drove through the Georgia countryside and into South Carolina, I found myself again seeing familiar scenery—the small frame homes and bare yards I had seen on my previous trips. I was reminded of Glen Allan. It seemed as if the South had so much in common throughout its territory.

During the long drive, Frances and I would take a break from listening to the NPR commentary and talk about books and the travesty of under-funding public education as we realized its importance to our democracy, but we didn't go that extra step and talk about the continued impact of race and place. Who better than the two of us to hold such a conversation? I should have led it, but somewhere along the highway, I had lost my will to bring it up as we sped past the inequities that still remained for all to see.

Frances turned the radio down a bit, and I leaned back into the car seat and dozed, but I sat up straight when the tires hit the first deep rut. We were now off the Old Allendale Road and onto the well-worn tree-lined dirt lane that led to Roselawn Plantation. I sat up straight as an arrow and looked around while Frances drove us into what I was now calling my "past with a purpose." Would I pick up where I had left off? Would I be able to respond to the servants as I had planned? I was anticipating something, but just what, I wasn't sure.

Just as I had been the first time, I was taken by Miss Camille's plantation home somehow survived both the nineteenth and twentieth centuries. It had not changed and was for all practical purposes in a world of its own. I was still apprehensive, but the intimidation was not as intense as before. And cotton was still growing everywhere. For others, the fields were just fields where cotton would be grown and harvested mechanically, but not so for me. I was unable to look at a cotton field without seeing the bent backs of my friends and kin stretched across the field, day in and day out.

Once more I felt like two people—Clifton Taulbert, the adult dinner guest, and Little Cliff, transported to the field to pick cotton. Frances, on the other hand, was still all smiles. She took the stately presence of the Low Country mansion in stride. It was simply a place where she once played. Unlike my first time with Mike and Kathy, Frances never slowed down to let me fully take in all the history I would be facing; she just nonchalantly drove to the back of the mansion and parked.

"Well, I got you here safe," she laughed. "Those were my orders—straight from Little Camille."

Frances was not one to be caught off guard. She had a quick wit. She did not miss one beat in our conversation as we made our way up to the back veranda. I listened and managed to laugh along with her as we talked. Inside my head, however, I was holding another conversation as we got closer to Miss Camille's welcoming door.

On the veranda, Frances didn't knock. Finally, I eased my way around her and knocked on the door. Obviously I had braved up. This meant I would be the person to greet the butler first. I had not forgotten my planned speech. I was ready. Hardly any time passed between my knock and the opening of the door. Only this time, instead of the colored help I expected, there was Little Camille.

We hugged and were ushered in to join those who had already arrived, including the veteran team members, the English and literature professors from Boston University, Assumption College, and several from the University of New Hampshire. While everyone was greeting us, I discreetly canvassed the room to see if I was the only black person present. Apparently I was. The lone black teacher from my first visit was not there, and I had yet to see the black help. While I was quietly surveying the other guests, Miss Camille appeared. Just as had happened when I first saw her, the small gathering in her beautiful home made way for her. She briskly walked across the room, nodding as she moved through the guests, and aimed her glance directly to where I was standing.

As natural as falling rain, she walked right to me, nodding at Frances. Just as she had in the lobby of the college, she leaned upward, gave me that familiar peck on the cheek, and welcomed me back to her home.

"Mister Taulbert, we are so glad to have you back with us. I was thrilled when Camille told me that you had been engaged."

I felt warmly welcomed, but inside I was expecting something different. Both Little Cliff and I knew from history what should have been her response. Instead, her actions toward me were still surprising at each turn.

The buzz and greetings around my safe arrival soon gave way to general conversation, including Karen Bohlin's worry over the airline losing her luggage, which naturally contained all her lecture materials. Little Camille assured her it would be delivered; Miss Camille was serenely unperturbed as she continued making sure that all of her guests were comfortable.

In the meantime, Little Cliff, not to be outdone, kept drawing my thoughts to the absence of the black teacher I had met when there before. I wanted to think that she had other things to do. But Little Cliff's voice in my head was now feeling vindicated and, as usual, cautioning me not to throw caution to the wind.

I told you so. If she couldn't come, they could have invited someone else. You know there is more than one black teacher in Allendale County. They made their point of inclusivity last time. There was no need to do it twice. Just remember, you are "back home" now, and things have not changed as much as you think.

MEANWHILE, MISS CAMILLE, as only she could do, ushered us into her dining room to another Southern supper. As we settled around the large antique table where we had eaten the previous year, I kept on the lookout for the black servers. Seated at the table and surrounded by all those artifacts of nineteenth-century Southern history, I felt that recognizable uneasiness settle upon me. My childhood was emerging and with it the culture of Glen Allan and the music that accompanied our people—the voices from our souls. Growing up amid people who embraced music as an integral part of their daily living, I had accepted this as part of my life as well. The uneasiness that I was feeling would not be calmed with a glass of imported wine, but with soulful humming. Yes, a song from back home is still my safe place, just as it once was for Mama Ponk.

Physically, I was at the table, but emotionally, I still had a ways to go.

Roselawn, with its beautiful antebellum trappings, was heavily laden with a history that had not included me in a positive way. That reality had always been a part of me, as well as the music that would move me through it. Just as before, there were no signs of the twenty-first century except for us seated around the table, which I knew was a far cry from what the Roselawn table would have looked like when the original owners and their friends were dining. I could only imagine whose feet had been under that same table and the conversations that ensued.

As we chatted and loaded our plates with food, I imagined white planters around this elegant table raising their glasses to toast a good crop of cotton or to celebrate an even greater sale, while their black servants—themselves bought and sold—stood silently by, waiting for orders. Yes, this was like Natchez's Melrose—a wonderful home for the landed gentry and those who would come after them. I was at the table, but I was not one of them.

As these thoughts raced through my head, it was as if I could sense the presence of Roselawn's past residents eyeing me and questioning my presence at their table—pointing me out to those seated around them—even as I looked to the head of the table where their descendant, Miss Camille, now sat. She was part of them, but that night she had stepped out of character. She had reached beyond their restrictions. She had invited me to place my feet under that same table.

This was indeed a roundtable that begged for conversation; I wondered if similar thoughts might have been in others' minds. It would have been a perfect time for each of us, as we toasted, to share our dream for the future of America, in which everyone was welcomed and every child was valued and surrounded with high expectations, as we would be teaching in our workshops.

Instead of leading such a conversation, I went with the flow. I blamed it on not wanting to interrupt the laughter and camaraderie with a heavy conversation. Yet I wondered if Miss Camille wanted such a conversation to take place. She never said so, but she never kept us from holding one. Could that be why she wrote me after my first presentation and why she came to my early morning workshop, when she didn't have to do either?

Then again, our reluctance to tackle the hard subjects and hold important conversations may have been due to Roselawn itself, an embodiment of the Old South. So instead of a roundtable conversation about the impact of the plantation system upon America, and upon me in particular, we gave in to the world that surrounded us. We bowed our heads as Miss Camille again offered grace. The evening wore on with much good Southern food, much good wine, much good talk and laughter. I joined in.

After supper, we dove into planning for the next day of professional development work for our assigned educators. Karen's lost luggage arrived. Our evening of talk and laughter continued for a while, and then we made ready to leave. As usual, Little Camille and her assistant, Rebecca Cupstid from the South Carolina Department of Education, were in charge of the housing assignments. With many of our assignments in small rural communities, housing was a challenge, but one item that Little Camille and her team met with promptness and confidence. We never had to be concerned about our lodgings.

As late as it was and as sleepy and filled with food and drink as we were, assigning rooms was another Southern production. Names were called, comments made, and instructions given to each person . . . twice. We all waited to see who would be lucky enough to stay at one of the few bed-and-breakfast inns; no one wanted the one-story motels where the doors opened to the parking lots. As I patiently listened, I also remembered that I was still in the rural South, and that I was the lone black male in our group. The lessons of race and place, male and black, were taught with such conviction by our elders that they still impact African Americans of my generation.

Boy, you best be careful when uptown. Step off the sidewalk when you see a white person walking towards you and 'specially so if it's a white woman. You hear me now, don't you?

Yes, I heard them then, and their admonitions were still loud and clear. Even though I was hundreds of miles from Glen Allan, Little Cliff could still see our one uptown main street and the white guys in their white T-shirts and beltless jeans, who fancied themselves the protectors of white women, leaning against their pickups and just waiting and watching for a black male to step out of line. In that world I knew to walk straight ahead and never to look around. I was taught to intentionally ignore them and to ignore white women at all costs.

Even in 2004, here in rural South Carolina, I never rested easy until at least one white guy was on my housing team. I was well aware of the complications that could arise if the person checking us in at the motel was one of those guys who still cherished the time when their words and actions were the rule and all matters of race were in their control. Also, I was mindful of the civil rights movement struggle just to ensure that black people could spend the night at any hotel or motel.

Nearly everybody was pretty much squared away when it dawned on me that my name had not been called. I had to get Little Camille's attention. "Camille, you forgot me. I'm over here," I said, as I anxiously looked around the room to make sure that I didn't sound as if I had been slighted—another lingering lesson of race and place. Being slighted and left out had also been a way of life for me and so many others whose lives were shaped by the same culture that shaped mine. I really didn't feel as if race was in play. However, I had to convince Little Cliff. He remembered yesterday, the way it used to be.

"Naw, I didn't forget you, Sugar. Just hold still for a minute. Now, you nice folks from New Hampshire, you two ladies right over there, you'll be staying here with Mama."

Their good fortune drew cheers. Roselawn was indeed the choice spot, even if I had to say so myself, but not a place I wanted to spend a night, surrounded by the ghosts of planters. All I needed was a nice room with plenty of people milling around in the lobby. So I waited as the very last name was called and still there was no assignment for me. I could feel Little Cliff stirring. This was a bit unusual. I wanted to raise my hands and wave them in the air, but I wasn't in the third grade. So I sort of raised one hand halfway and cleared my throat loudly—a man can do that and not be chastised for doing so.

"Honey, just hold your horses," Little Camille said. "I haven't forgotten you. You're staying right here with Mama!" Her voice was matter-of-fact and final.

There was more cheering; from the others' vantage point, I had just won the sleep-over lottery. But Little Cliff was not cheering. While such an opportunity could be viewed as a moment of triumph on behalf of all those who looked like me and all those who had labored to make this plantation a reality, I had no desire to be the lone black male sleeping in the same Southern mansion as white women, regardless of their ages. We were in the rural South, way off the main pathway, where time in some respects seemed to have stood still. Sure, it was 2004, but Little Cliff was snatching me back to 1955, to another small town, Money, Mississippi, where an innocent whistle (if he actually whistled) had precipitated the tragic murder of Emmett Till. His mutilation and murder became the lesson that we all learned well—*no matter what happens, ignore white women.*

I didn't know how to share my honest feelings. I didn't want them to know that a scared little black boy lived inside the tall, well-dressed black man. This was my personal burden, the lingering harsh lessons from the era of legal segregation and the legacy of slavery. Many people feel that the civil rights movement made everything right and should have automatically erased our memory of all that we had endured, as well as the lessons of race and place we had been systematically taught. I knew that for me and most

African Americans, no matter how high we had risen, it wasn't that simple.

The past is never quite past. Although I was barely ten when Emmett Till was murdered, I remembered how the horrific way he was killed had taken on a life of its own in my colored community. He became everybody's visiting cousin. He became every aunt's nephew and every grandmother's grandson. As the story grew, so did the widening gap between whites and blacks. His murder may not have been embraced by the whole of the white community, but for some it spoke of their power and our place.

All of this came back to me that evening at Roselawn. Though surrounded by good people, highly educated, and by all accounts committed to social justice, I felt alone and trapped by history. My head was ignoring all the positive change around me. The warm handshake from Miss Camille I had encountered years earlier didn't seem to matter. Her visit to my workshop was almost forgotten in that moment. It was crazy how my mind responded to what would have been exciting and natural for others. The past is indeed powerful, and this invitation was taking me further into that past.

I needed to get this resolved, and quickly. Little Camille, of course, was standing in the middle of her mother's den with no look of concern on her face. From her perspective, there was no problem. The Civil War was over and Jim Crow was history.

There was no way I would tell her what was actually inside my head. So I covered my real frustrations with a more easily shared if not nearly so compelling truth—my snoring. "Camille, thank you, but please, you don't have to go out of your way for me. Let one of the other first-time guys stay here. I'd just as soon stay at one of the local motels—plus, they say I snore something awful."

She was not buying. "Clifton, most folks snore, but life tends to go on. You'll be just fine here. The walls are 'thick as time' in this house. Mama requested you. You've been around Mama for some time now and you know that what Mama wants, Mama gets."

Meanwhile, her mother stood quietly, looking on. She never said a word. Her quietness told me that she had arranged this ahead of time. Who had I become to Miss Camille? Had I reminded her of someone from her past, as she had reminded me of Miss Jeffries? She knew that her invitation was reshaping the social South we both knew. Why was she doing this? With all the Southern charm I could muster, I tried to get Miss Camille to rethink her invitation.

The small woman with the big stature was not buying, either. "Mister Taulbert, it's all settled. Everybody has a place to stay, and your room is through those doors right over there. Now don't let all us crazy white women scare you; you'll have your privacy."

"Well, I just thought—."

Before I could say more, Little Camille chimed in. "No need to think, Sugar. It's all settled."

AND SO IT WAS. The evening at Roselawn ended. There was nothing left for me to do except get my stuff from Frances's trunk and watch as the others drove off into the night, leaving me standing alone, looking at a Southern mansion partially surrounded by cotton fields. With the last taillight out of view, I made my back up the stairs to the veranda. The door was open. It was rather strange just walking up and opening the screen door as if I lived there. This time I didn't have to knock. I just walked in, closing the door behind me. The two ladies had gone to their rooms, and, as hard as I had looked, I had yet to see the black help. Somehow, I was glad. I didn't want them to see me staying in the house they had to clean. It may have meant nothing to them. To me, though, it was something to think about.

The den where diverse voices had blended in laughter just minutes earlier was now silent except for clean-up sounds coming from the kitchen. Words from one of our church hymns tried to find a place alongside of me as I stood and waited. *Troubles don't last always.*

For a few seconds, it was just me, time, the history I remembered, and the history being made, all standing together in the quiet den of an antebellum mansion. While I waited for Miss Camille, Little Cliff was still in a time warp, back in Glen Allan at Linden, another Southern plantation home. The majestic white pillars that supported its front portico were so real that I felt I could reach out and touch them. I could see the swell of beautiful Lake Washington, which the local whites led us to believe was owned by them, fronting this beautiful home where a prominent white Southern family lived and black Southerners worked. Even the ancient magnolia trees of Linden, which looked as if they bore the weight of the centuries upon each expanding branch, crowded into my head. For a while, I was a little boy again.

When my great-grandmother died, I became my great-aunt's charge. I called her Mama Ponk. Wherever she went, I followed. So it wasn't unusual for me to have trailed her to the Linden Plantation, where she was the day cook. I thought we would never get there, but Mama Ponk kept urging me to keep up, and I did. We finally arrived at Linden. Being there was exciting for a young boy. The plantation yard was filled with activity as black workers gathered to start the day in the massive yard, canopied by ancient trees, waiting for orders from those in charge. After Mama Ponk got her orders, I was allowed to follow her into the main house to the kitchen, where I was told to stay put and keep out of the way.

Somehow during the early part of her workday, I wandered from the area that was designated for black workers. I was too young to know this. I was just inquisitive. I took off in the direction of the highly polished wood floor that led to the owners' elegant living quarters. I was just an innocent but nosy little boy who thought he had the run of the house. Even though every step I made was magic, I was somehow smart enough not to open closed doors. So I prowled the halls peeking only in rooms where the doors were opened wide.

One bedroom had its door open. I had never seen such a room. The walls were covered with wallpaper that I now know captured breathtaking French scenes. The bed was massive, bigger than both beds in our small bedroom at home. I could barely take my eyes off its canopy which almost touched the ceiling. I had never seen such a bed. I remember standing in the doorway staring. Bright colors were everywhere. I now know them to have been silk, brocade, and lace bed linens. I learned this from articles that were eventually written about this home. The room bore no resemblance to our small bedroom where we had an iron double bed and my wood-framed cot, which sat by the front windows with just enough room left for the washstand. The other wall held up our chifforobe, the freestanding wardrobe that held all our clothes, and, next to the wardrobe, our wood-burning stove.

I'm not sure how long I stood and ogled, but after some time Mama Ponk had apparently realized that she had no earthly idea where I was. I had been told to stay within her sight, which of course I had not done. She couldn't leave the kitchen, so she sent one of the other female helpers to find me. I don't know who she was or what she did, but obviously the young woman finally found me standing in the doorway of the bedroom. Without a moment's hesitation, I recall her grabbing me by the arm and dragging me back to the world beyond the highly polished wood floors, quietly but firmly setting me straight as she went.

"Boy, you must be some crazy. Don't you ever let them catch you up here. Yore place is in the back wid us."

Early on, I was introduced to "them." They were the white owners. In that moment, as in others that would follow, I was reminded and shown my place in broader society. I left the Mississippi Delta at seventeen, but by then, I was well aware of the difference between "them and us." It became one of the many indelible lessons that followed my life's journey. It was reinforced on the Illinois Central, the train I took from Greenville, Mississippi, as I headed north. The "colored" porter kindly showed me my place in the "colored" train car. I wasn't in Glen Allan anymore, but the same rules applied to my life.

Yes, Little Cliff remembered the lesson from Linden Plantation, one of many lessons of "them and us" that would follow me throughout my life. As I waited, those lingering lessons were welling up inside me. I had no idea how this night would go. I had to wait and see. There were now no cheerful educators to buffer Little Cliff and me from our history. I had no lecture to deliver. We would be on our own.

I LISTENED ANXIOUSLY FOR any sound coming from the kitchen that would bring me back to the twenty-first century. It was now nearly midnight. I couldn't imagine why it was taking Miss Camille so long. I had never seen any black help and decided she must have used caterers; surely they would have cleaned up.

Finally, Miss Camille's voice broke through the uneasy silence, calling out to me. "Mister Taulbert, you think you want a bedtime snack?"

She was offering me more food. It was almost midnight and she was offering me more food. I politely said, "No, thank you." Besides I was too nervous to eat or drink anything.

With that settled, I could hear her soft footsteps as she walked from the kitchen into the den. There was no telltale sign of uneasiness on her face. I was still assessing—and stressing—but she looked completely calm. Had she really moved on beyond the racial divide? What was holding me back?

"Well, sir, it's time for bed. I'll show you to your quarters. It's all private, you know. You don't have to be embarrassed about all the women here. They have their bath on their side. You won't even know we are here," she said while looking me squarely in the face, not batting an eye.

Hearing her say "I'll show you to your quarters" made me think even more about Glen Allan and other small Southern towns with their colored "quarters." Even during slavery, the "quarters" often referred to the collection of small wood-framed shack homes where the black workers lived. Having never slept in a Southern mansion before, maybe the use of "quarters" was commonplace among the mansion dwellers as well.

America had changed. The South was changing, even though the lessons of our collective pasts still lingered. I knew a conversation between us was needed, but she just smiled a smile that said, *It's all settled. Let me get you to your room.* As she turned to the small dimly lit hallway that led to what she had warmly called "my quarters," I followed her into a world that I had only read about or watched from a distance when I was a child—inside the world of "them." Although I felt her invitation to be heartfelt, I could not easily move from "us" to "them." Little Cliff, well aware of the world of my youth and the social restrictions I had known, was there beside me, reminding me that my literary and professional accomplishments took the backseat to my segregated past, which that night was standing tall.

I was tired, not just because I needed sleep, but because of all the conversations that had gone though my head. I expected my stay at Roselawn to be different, but I did not expect it to be so powerful.

I wish I knew what had caused Miss Camille to extend this invitation to me. Why was it important for me to be a guest at her home? Was she sending a message to the others? I don't know. We never talked about the invitation. That night, however, it didn't really matter. She had orchestrated the evening and I had no choice but to go along. Besides, all the other team members were gone, I had no car, and we were far from the rest of the world.

9

Invisible People

"I am an invisible man. No, I am not a spook like those who haunted Edgar Allan Poe; nor am I one of your Hollywood-movie ectoplasms. I am a man of substance, of flesh and bone, fiber and liquids—and I might even be said to possess a mind. I am invisible, understand, simply because people refuse to see me."
—*Ralph Waldo Ellison*, Invisible Man

WHAT A SIGHT WE MUST HAVE BEEN: AN AGING WHITE FEMALE plantation owner, a small off-white dog, and me, the black man from Glen Allan, preparing to call it a day. I followed as Miss Camille led the way, moving with ease through the antiques in her home on what for me was a slow-motion walk through history. Silence surrounded us. She paused to turn off a lamp; then we went on.

This was the twenty-first century, but, surrounded by the trappings of the Old South, I was very cognizant of all that had separated our lives. She was the daughter of planters. I was the son of field hands. Perhaps this would have been a good time to share with her how being surrounded by her past made me feel. Instead, I said nothing and neither did she.

As we approached what she referred to as my "quarters," she spoke up: "I've made everything ready for you. I sure hope you find your accommodations to your liking."

"'I'm sure it'll be fine, thank you," I replied quietly. Really, there was little else I could say. I heard her say *I have made everything ready for you.* Now I was sure that inviting me to stay over had been a premeditated decision. My trepidation would have made no difference at all.

I could feel the reality of the twenty-first century jockeying for position in my thinking, but the past—those lingering lessons of race and place—was powerful. The best I could do was try to walk a path between both worlds as this daughter of the Old South escorted me through the stately mansion to the guest quarters she had prepared for me. Miss Camille had forewarned me about the creaking of the planks in the original wooden flooring, which added eeriness to the uneasiness I was feeling in the silent old house. All the while, she was still holding onto my arm, moving with confidence in her world while bringing me along.

I physically moved alongside her, but my mind had moved backwards to the 1960s when, throughout the South, young black men and women were marching and staging sit-ins and being jailed, just so that they could be recognized as equal citizens under the law. I doubt if securing the rights for "sleepovers" at private Southern mansions was among their motivations. Their focus was on public accommodations. The Carolinas, like my home state of Mississippi, were among the places where the past collided with the future before the eyes of the world. Those courageous young men and women wanted America to live up to its creed, and public accommodation was their first strike. Maybe that is why I found it slightly easier in the integrated college setting where Miss Camille and I first crossed paths. That was a public place, but this was her home, where before tonight I would have felt the "off limits" signs would surely be posted forever.

No such signs were posted at Roselawn. What was on the hallway walls surrounding us as we walked were family pictures. As we passed them, as if I needed to know and she needed to tell me, she shared memories and facts about her life prompted by these portraits.

Meanwhile, I was having my own internal tour of her past. I had not thought in a long time of the three young African American students, Ronald Martin, Robert Patterson, and Mark Martin, who were depicted in a famous photograph of them seated at the Woolworth's lunch counter in Greensboro, North Carolina. That picture has become an icon of the sit-in movement (launched the day before, February 1, 1960, by Ezell Blair Jr., David Richmond, Franklin McCain, and Joseph McNeil). While those young men and the young men and women who followed their lead took brave steps, I was still in high school in Greenville, Mississippi, hardly aware that they were forever changing the landscape of my world. Today, however, I am fully aware of their resolve, and I am certain that as they marched, chanted, and sat-in in the 1960s they were not imagining being invited to a Southern plantation for supper and to spend the night.

NOT FAR FROM THE end of our walk, near the opening to the small hall by the front bedroom—my quarters—we came to an exquisite oil painting of a beautiful young lady. Captivating with its bright colors of yellow and red, the picture seemed out-of-place among all those of stern-faced men and women. I stopped to stare at it. Miss Camille remained quiet for a moment, and then spoke up warmly and reflectively.

"That's me when I was a young woman, so many, many years ago."

Wow. She was beautiful.

I didn't think it appropriate to say so out loud. Some recognizable voice from yesterday was saying, *"Don't go there."* I should have paid her that compliment—at her age, why not?—but, with Little Cliff in my ear, I said nothing; in his world of my youth, such innocent thoughts and compliments were not to be forthcoming from "us" to "them," nor expected from "them" to "us."

So another conversation was passed by. I suppose she also sensed that expectant but lost opportunity, for in a moment she said, "You know, I've had a good life."

Her statement came out of the blue and hit me directly in the face. I was surprised at how matter-of-factly she said it. I had assumed that her life had been good. All I had to do was to look around me at the elegance that was hers by birth. Was she acknowledging how my life and the lives of those who had cared for me may have been? Our worlds were indeed a study in contrast—the planter and the worker, the mansion and the sharecropper's home. She had made a statement, one that begged for elaboration, but I didn't think she expected a follow-up from me. We walked on. After a few long moments, she surprised me again.

"I went to college, you know."

I could sense the pride in her voice as she casually told me that she had gone to college. Her educational background was something I had not thought of. At the time, I could not understand why it had become an important statement to make, near midnight during a slow stroll through Roselawn's portrait gallery. But I could see in her eyes that it was important to her that I know that she was a college lady.

I understood that was telling me more than my ears heard. But what and why, I will never know. Thinking back to that night, I have often wondered if some college experience had somehow given her a different perspective of her life. Maybe she had met someone or had a class where the way of life she had known had been challenged. Or maybe it was her show of independence, a woman going off to school when it would have been just as easy to stay home and marry well. I should have asked her about those college days, but it was late and the night was already like no other in my life. I wanted a stimulating intellectual discourse, but the journey to it was down a path that was familiar, necessary, and also forbidden.

We fell quiet for a moment, but not the old floor. It creaked and squeaked with each step. If only those planks could have talked to me. I could have asked what they had observed in a home that was so closely related to our history of slavery and Jim Crow segregation. I wanted those stories, but I dared not ask my hostess about the inhumanity that inevitably went along with the elegance that surrounded us.

JUST DOWN THE HALL from my room, a small black and white picture hanging over a little antique table in the dimly lit hallway caught my eye. I felt compelled to get a closer look. I felt as if it had some power of suggestion, pulling me to it. I gently dropped Miss Camille's arm and leaned toward it. I waited for her to say something. Instead she remained exactly where we had stopped, with her hands to her side, with no explanation. I knew she was watching me.

As a child, stories told by older relatives about midnight ghosts took on the validity of historic fact. However, I guess I was educated out of superstitious beliefs. Their reality had died off with the elders who had made their presence seem so real with passionate late-night stories. This night at Roselawn I suddenly felt as if I was back in Poppa's front room where the kerosene lamplights cast shadows across the walls and the storytellers' voices took little kids to beyond the world in which we lived. I was reliving such a night. I could swear before my elders that the small photograph possessed a power beyond my understanding; maybe my elders knew of this world.

I leaned down and gazed into the late nineteenth- or very early twentieth-century black-and-white photograph of several white people. They were well-dressed men with women in long dresses, standing tall at the edge of a cotton field, with their horses and buggies behind them. This scene was not out of the ordinary. Roselawn was a cotton plantation that had been owned by generations of white people. Yet I felt that pull—that surreal feeling of something going on beyond the ordinary. I couldn't walk away. Miss Camille was quietly watching as I peered into the photograph as deeply as any human could. Seeing nothing that affected me, I was ready to turn away when my eyes seemingly moved of their own accord from the white people posing in the foreground to the very back of the photograph, deep in the cotton field. There I recognized the distant images of black fieldworkers, their postures forever bent and frozen in time.

I knew that bent pose. It had been my own. I could imagine the music coming from their souls. I knew they would be singing, or quietly humming if someone in authority was around. But if no bosses were present, their voices would reach the sky. In my day, the singing across the fields lightened our hard labor and cushioned our souls from the intimidating voices of the straw bosses, usually white men, hired to watch us. I imagined the bent figures in this photograph to be doing likewise, with words like *Hush, hush, somebody calling my name* ringing out across the fields. This is what we did in Glen Allan, not so many years ago. Our true feelings and cautious sayings were well-hidden within the words that danced from our lips. Though the white subjects of the photo, or the photographer, never saw or heard the bent figures, I knew their souls were singing their troubles.

That particular framed photograph had lifted me to another place, one where *we* were the only ones present. That one picture spoke more than its thousand words. It told me the story of our historic presence in America, and the lack of value accorded to us. It was Ralph Ellison's *Invisible Man* come alive in my presence.

If I could have, I would have walked into that framed photograph, to lift their bodies from their frozen position of servitude to a posture of standing tall. I wanted so badly to tell them that life had changed and that the cries of their hearts had not gone unheard. I wanted to tell them that I was spending the night in the type of house their labor had helped to build. I wanted to share with them the heart-wrenching words of Dr. King's speeches and writings, where he so powerfully aligned himself, and all of us, with them—the invisible people, the real workforce—fully recognizing that they had been unable to benefit from the fruits of their labor, but also that they had not been forgotten. Our living would vindicate theirs. I wanted to climb into the photograph and stand beside them and tell them about Jake Ayers from Glen Allan, an ordinary man whose life bore scars from standing tall for our people. I wanted to tell them about how he had been beaten by the Ku Klux Klan because he stood up for equal, quality education for children and young people who looked like me. They tried to break him. They didn't. He won! I wish I could have told them about Jake. Though generations removed, he was still their boy. Because Jake won, they did as well. I wanted them to know that their soul-rending cries had not gone unheard in this world or in heaven. Their soulful and mournful singing had become the prayers that fueled our movements for social, economic, and political justice.

I wanted to show them the photograph of that young black preacher, Martin Luther King, who had said and written those words I referred to, and tell them more, even, about Selma and the march on Washington and about his Nobel Peace Prize and, sadly, about his assassination. He has been called Atlanta's native son, but he was their boy as well. One of their own had helped change the world.

Fieldwork was back-breaking. And for many it was the only source of income they could aspire to; the planters' world had sought to keep them in a bent position. The fieldworkers in that photograph were well accustomed to sitting in the back and not being served up front—or at all—and maybe felt that such injustices would last forever. It was the only life they had ever known. I wanted them to know Miss Fannie Lou Hamer, who, like them, was a cotton picker. She had spent much of her life in the same bent posture but one day straightened up and on behalf of our people walked right out of the cotton fields of the Delta to the Democratic National Convention. There were many other heroes they needed to hear about.

And if I could, I would tell them that the lessons of survival they had learned and taught to their children had continued to be passed along, even to my generation. Though I was no longer in a stooped position of servitude, I still heard the voices of my elders cautioning me not to throw caution to the wind. I was still very aware of what our color had dictated from the start of slavery to this present day. I had a rush of sadness as I realized that I, too—of all people—almost missed seeing them. *Are we this invisible to the world around us?* The picture had not been taken to preserve their images or their presence. The focus was on those who mattered—the owners of the land—not on those who worked the land and who looked like me. Yet they were there all the time, living on the outskirts of the world that surrounded them.

Maybe for the first time in my life, I really came to grips with Ralph Ellison's *Invisible Man.* I knew the book. I had studied it in college and, intellectually, I understood all that Ellison was saying: Our presence had not mattered, our intellectual capacity had been questioned (or denied) and our ability to be sought-after partners was not even considered. Seeing that one small, black-and-white framed photograph made it crystal clear for me. You are indeed invisible when your presence is simply part of a backdrop, nothing more and nothing less.

Even more telling is the idea that this reality of being invisible to others could have been so pervasive that many of us may not have seen *ourselves.* It helped me to understand so much more about being left out, even while supposedly at the table, as in those moments when I needed to speak up among peers, but remained quiet, having value to add but questioning its worth when surrounded by others who looked different from me. How many times had I been overlooked as I almost overlooked the bent figures in that photo? How many times had I overlooked *myself?*

I could feel tears welling up. I clenched my fists and held the tears back. To have cried then, in Miss Camille's presence, might have unleashed an untimely conversation. But that night I clearly saw the divide that in their time was so commonplace and still shows up in my life, and that Little Cliff is keenly aware of.

My people. Me. We were there all the time, toiling away, half bent over, and trying desperately to hide from the searing sun. But we did eventually stand up. How could the fieldworkers in the old photo have known that despite the lingering lessons of race and place, our lives *did* change. This night at Roselawn Plantation, I understood how far we had come and how much further we had to go.

I HAD SEEN WHAT I needed to see. I could feel Miss Camille's presence at my back, waiting with the little dog. Did she know what I had seen? Or had she always overlooked the bent figures, as I almost had? I stepped back from the picture and looked around to her. She smiled and again graciously extended her arm toward my mine. With my luggage occupying one arm and Miss Camille on the other, we continued.

At the door to my room, she interrupted the silence and the walk with another unexpected conversation. "My sweet mother died when I was just a child. My daddy had his hands full. One of the black women who worked for us, our maid, Mary, helped to raise me and got me through that awful time in my life."

She didn't elaborate. I know something else was behind her brief but heartfelt comment, but I also knew I had heard all that she would say for now. Hearing her speak of kindness from those "forever stooped" souls was conflicting, but that whole era was conflicting. Our South is, indeed, very complicated, with levels of emotions that are difficult to understand and even more difficult to explain.

I wondered about her relationship with that black woman. She was just a child then, but just as I had to learn to be "colored," she had to learn to be "white." I wanted to know more about the Mary who had taken care of her. I have always been intrigued by black women who could love little white kids as if they were their own. In most cases, up to certain ages, that love was requited. I had seen this in my own life. My mother had been a maid in the Delta, and the two white kids that she cared for would scream their little heads off to follow my mother home. They responded to her love for them. As they grew older, someone had to teach them to use "color" to temper their natural response. I just wondered how it had been with Miss Camille.

I wanted to know how she had felt about the cotton world that had surrounded her life and the people who populated her childhood world. She had heard two lectures from me and had read *Once Upon a Time When We Were Colored* and even knew the names of my elders; I had been very forthcoming about my segregated world. I named names. I shared personal anecdotes, both funny and hurtful. But up to this point, I knew little or nothing about the character of the people who had shaped her life. What was her father's name and where had they come from? Who were her aunts and uncles? And who were the black people who moved in and out of her life? But I was her guest, not a journalist.

That night, upon seeing our shared reality framed in black and white, I could not stop the rising tide of hurt. At the same time, I was careful not to make any missteps. I wanted the revolution, and I wanted the peace treaty. Although Miss Camille upon our first meeting had unwittingly reminded me of much of what I wanted to forget, her actions toward me had been far different than I expected. Warned by familiar inner voices not to throw caution to the wind, I took her graciousness in stride. I was uncertain that I could read her, but I was always left surprised. Her place, her Southern home, steeped in its pre-Civil War history, demanded the conversation I wanted so badly to hold. I wanted to know the depth of her feelings about me and those who looked like me. Other than the brief comment about the maid who cared for her, and her squeeze of my arm that followed, there was no further talk that night about relationships between the races.

The oversized wooden door to my room was before us—a door that once separated our lives. The short walk from Miss Camille's den to what she called my quarters had been a walk through decades and centuries, taking me down roads I had needed to travel. Realizing what lay beyond the massive door, I mustered my will to make it through that night. I could not turn back. I was where I was going. I knew this, as did Little Cliff.

Miss Camille's arm dropped from mine; I had to go through the door by myself. I stepped aside as she placed her small hand on the doorknob and made several quick turns. I waited as the old and ancient door slowly opened wide.

10

Once Forbidden

"History, despite its wrenching pain, cannot be unlived, but if faced with courage, need not be lived again." —Maya Angelou

THE LONG NIGHT'S JOURNEY WAS ALMOST OVER. WITH THE big wooden door opened wide, I could see fully what as a young black boy I had been scolded for innocently venturing into. Surely no prior guest in this great house ever felt more out of place. Little Cliff was certainly well aware of where he was. However, this time, no one was there to pull on my arm and remove me. It was all right to be in these quarters. I had been invited.

Miss Camille was quiet. Maybe she understood some of what was going on in my head, even though she had not asked why I had almost been knocked to my knees by the little framed photograph in the hallway. Finally, Miss Camille turned on the crystal chandelier and the bedroom came to life. And there it stood, the large canopied bed, almost reaching to the ceiling.

Oh, man, am I sleeping in this bed?

This was the world our labor had helped to build. Sleeping here . . . is this not what I wanted? I should have been elated—feeling vindicated from my childhood experience at Linden Plantation. Instead, Little Cliff and the adult I had become were caught in a collision of two worlds: the past we both knew and the present I was trying to embrace. With a deep breath, I tried to take it all in. As I stood amid the grandeur of the Old South, Miss Camille quietly watched. I felt she must have understood my uneasiness, but instead of going in this direction, she dove into talking about the history of the room, all the furniture, and, again, her relatives, as if they were my own. I listened, but my head was elsewhere. I wanted to know why I was invited.

Next she opened the door to the bathroom and led me in. I know she realized what she was doing, even though she didn't make conversation about the "White" or "Colored" signs we were both familiar with from past years. It all felt right, but were her gracious acts just coincidental—her way of treating everyone—or was she responding to her own internal conversation about race and place?

The bedroom was antebellum, but the bathroom was modern. Everything I would need had been set out. When she opened the door to the large walk-in shower, for a brief moment, I felt as if all was well with the world and that I no longer had to worry about throwing caution to the wind. This was one of those moments when a song, slowly and soulfully rendered, would express my feelings. With a song, I could laugh or cry and not have to render an explanation. The voice of Billie Holiday played in my head. *God bless the child who has his own.* I am still defining "my own" and the process was in full swing that night. I realized that I was in another person's world. But I was not jealous of all that I was seeing and all that Miss Camille was showing me. It's just that the difference in our two worlds was so apparent. It seemed unfathomable that this big guest suite at Roselawn would be "my own" for the night.

"Mister Taulbert," said Miss Camille, "if you are like my grandson Carl, you are going to mess up a load of towels. Now right over there in that corner is an extra stack just in case you need them."

Of course, I thanked her, but it wasn't the extra towels that got my attention. It was her comparing me to her grandson, Carl, whom I had met. This was not the conversation Little Cliff anticipated, and, quite frankly, neither did the adult Clifton. I know something important to both our lives was going on in her mind, but we had no conversation to clarify what it was. When she had covered all she felt I needed to know, she walked me back into the bedroom where, once again, the antebellum elegance with the memory of the framed photograph made me keenly aware of the difference in race and place that was, and in some instances still remains, in spite of my having just been compared to her blonde-haired grandson.

She knew the circumstances of my growing up years, but never once did I sense that she was starting a conversation, or building some bridge of understanding about the past, or expressing regret about the different lifestyles we had experienced. At the same time, she never made me feel as if I was lucky to be there. Things were matter-of-fact as she went along. Maybe without saying it, we both knew that our different pasts had simply been the luck of the draw—over which neither of us had control. The small wooden cot that was my childhood bed was not a choice I made. It was part of the way of life that greeted me at birth. And I know the life she had enjoyed had not been because of a choice she made. We were both products of the world that surrounded us.

Along the way, though, there were brave men and women who were not content to let that status quo stand forever against our shared humanity and the national documents that called for human equality. Our separate worlds had been merged by the heroes of the civil rights movement, and Miss Camille and I knew their struggles had played a great role in the invitation that she had extended.

WITH THE OTHER GUESTS no doubt snoring away in the comforts of their own antebellum beds, it was time for Miss Camille and me to call it a night—a night that had become more memorable by the minute. Miss Camille had shown me every little thing, in full detail. But as she and her posse of one, the little off-white dog, turned to leave, she stopped. She just tiptoed a bit and as if I was indeed her grandson gave me a quick peck on the cheek, then turned to walk away.

Suddenly she turned around, and this time in the place of the familiar smile was an unfamiliar scowl. I was stunned. I had certainly done nothing to bring that look on, but it was there nonetheless. There was no doubt that she had something important to say.

Here it comes now—the talk about race.

It was late. As much as I wanted this talk, I wasn't fully prepared to hold it. Yet I was suddenly sure that she had been thinking about what she would say since our paths first crossed in the college auditorium. I watched as the tense and angry words were pushed out.

"Mister Taulbert, can you imagine . . . ?"

I was shocked at how adamant she was. Her tone of voice made her appear to be at least a foot taller. Before I could answer the half-question, she continued in the same angry breath—small and tall and defiant all at the same time.

"This very room right here, the one that you will be sleeping in, was used by the Union Army during the war."

I was shocked. Was this what she wanted to tell me? Race and place I wanted to discuss with her, not the Civil War—and certainly not as if I would be a Southern sympathizer. She had just compared me to her grandson and provided me with extra thick towels . . . and now she had on her battle face and it sounded as if I was being invited to be loyal to the Confederacy. It came out of left field for me, but not for her. The intensity on her face said it all. She was still mad as hell about something that had happened a century and a half ago. I had nowhere to go other than to stand firm and hear her out. Surely she knew that it was the Union Army that set in motion the freeing of the slaves—my people. Somehow that fact seemed to have gotten lost. I could tell she expected my complete understanding of whatever was to come next.

"Mister Taulbert, this is where that awful General Judson Kilpatrick set up his headquarters—right here in my family's home."

I honestly had no idea what to say. First, I had no notion who this general was and what he had done during the 1860s, other than occupying her home. Her face was still tense. Her eyes were no longer sparkling. She was in a different time. I could see that. She had traveled back to the lifetime of Judson Kilpatrick, born in 1836 in New Jersey as Hugh Judson Kilpatrick. He later dropped the Hugh when attending the United States Military Academy, the start of his military career, and assumed a command during the Civil War.

Stunned, I continued to listen, with no idea how I, a black Southerner, would deal with my hostess's antagonism toward the memory of this general, whose actions remained a thorn in her flesh.

"Besides being a Yankee, he had a horrible personal reputation, almost a man without honor. The nerve to call himself a general! Do you know, it is highly rumored, and I believe every word of it, that while here, he also kept several women for his personal pleasure."

I did not see this coming . . . women for his pleasure. Yes, I knew exactly her reference, and what it entailed then and now, but I was not about to go there. Not only was she a grandmother figure, but—growing up when and where I did—I could never imagine any subject closely related to sex ever being discussed between whites and blacks of any age. I just looked up into the chandelier while she continued.

"Can you imagine that? This house was built by my great-grandfather, Reverend Joseph Alexander Lawton. That scoundrel Kilpatrick showed no respect at all, not one bit of respect."

By now, I was beginning to get it. This had nothing to do with the Civil War and North-South differences. This had to do with her concept of civility—doing what was right regardless of the situation. Now I was getting a picture of how she may have been raised. What had the black maid taught her? What had her father taught her? Why had she insisted on choosing me instead of one of the white team members who would have loved to be her guest at Roselawn? Why was it important to tell me about this general and his lack of respect for her family? I will never be quite sure why we had that conversation.

"He just moved them to a far back room with an outside entrance. They may have well been sequestered out back. He took them away from their room and their comfort."

She let out a deep breath. Of course, whether she realized it or not, she was telling my story as well—a people taken from their own land and moved out back, as it were. It was uncanny how we both were moved by the lack of respect that our kin had suffered at the hands of others.

I was not able to share her anger over a Union general's lack of respect, but I understood her anger that no one had come to the rescue of her kin. I had harbored plenty of such anger myself. Sometimes a hundred and fifty years ago can seem like yesterday. I know this. Little Cliff knows this. I have my stories. Miss Camille had hers. Listening and not really commenting was by far the best thing that I could have done that night. She continued, though not in the same bristled and angry tone as before.

"On the other hand, God does work in mysterious ways. His being here and all his doings no doubt saved this house from utter destruction. I'm absolutely sure that Sherman would have demanded it be burned to a bacon crisp. You know, Mister Taulbert, since it was first built in the early 1840s, only our family has occupied this home." I celebrated and envied her unbroken link to her history. Maybe for the moment she had forgotten I had no such link.

So in the end, Miss Camille had found some good in the situation that had traveled with her for all her life. No, she had not forgiven the general, but she found that in his unethical behavior, her home had been spared. I later read up on the general and discovered that his flaws had ruffled feathers on both sides during the war.

Unlike Miss Camille, I wasn't a child of the Confederacy—a Southerner yes, but not a child of the Confederacy. We would probably always see that war through different lenses, but that's all right. It's another day now and we can wear lenses of our own making—lenses that would allow an aging white planter to compare her black guest to her grandson and lenses that would allow a black writer, though shadowed by his past, to extend his arm to an aging white planter, making sure that she made no missteps while walking.

THE CONVERSATION THAT INVOKED the Civil War came to an end, finally. The smile had returned to her face. As she moved toward the door, she stopped to point out, again, the nightlight along the baseboard. "Mister Taulbert, I always keep this small light on." In her thoughtfulness, she also pointed to a couple of magazines to read in case I had trouble going to sleep. She had thought of everything, almost.

The invitation itself would remain a mystery. I just know that Miss Camille acted as if she had been expecting me all along, as if she knew that one day I would show up. Acknowledging the nightlight, I was ready to say goodnight, but Miss Camille would have the last words.

"Now, Mr. Taulbert, you've got all you need. Just close your door and no one will disturb you. I'll see you at breakfast in the morning. Do you need anything else?"

"Miss Camille, everything is just fine."

She gave me a gentle pat on the hand and walked from my room with her dog at her heels.

Left alone, I stood for a second and looked at the magnificent, hand-carved, lace-canopied bed. This was indeed a strange night. I thought of the bent figures in the photograph and my people in Glen Allan and knew what their accommodations would have been: no ruffles, no lace, barely enough room to sleep. I could only imagine the white Southerners who had stood where I was standing as they made ready for bed. Had General Kilpatrick actually slept in this very bed or just in this room? Thinking back on what

Miss Camille had said about his personal pleasure, I laughed to myself and shook my head.

But first things first. I made my way to the bathroom and cleaned up, making sure that I left everything spotless behind me. I had experienced a full day and an even fuller night. I remembered again the comforting words that had eased us through the challenging routine of our yesterdays: *Maybe troubles don't last always.*

With the quietness came all the memories I had held at bay. The hallway and the small dimly lit photograph. The bent backs frozen in time. The off-limits bathroom in Mr. Hilton's store. The off-limits bedroom at Linden Plantation. All the lessons of "them and us" that lingered with me.

The memories in my head were so real and continuous that I knew sleep would be my only rescue. So I literally climbed up into the tall antebellum bed with the aid of a small step-stool, slid under the white sheet, and wished that the people in the photograph could have had just one night in this room that their labor had helped to purchase. Then I gave in to the sounds in my head—Mama Mae, my great-aunt, singing her fourth Sunday special: *'Tis that Old Ship of Zion, it has safely landed many a thousands.* The Saint Mark's Baptist Church would be enraptured as Mama Mae stood in the choir loft and belted out that we had a room on the ship.

I curled up, recalling her song of promise inviting us to get on board to go to this other place. She never imagined the ship would dock at Roselawn, and when I was a child, neither had I. As Mama Mae's singing faded in my mind, I found sleep and even rest in a bed and in a room that was once forbidden.

11

On the Inside, Looking Out

"I am a part of all that I have seen." —Alfred Lord Tennyson

I AWOKE WITH THE SUN SHINING IN MY FACE, SAT UP IN BED, and looked around at the antique-filled room that had been mine, if only for the night. I was not dreaming, but given my surroundings, it would not be difficult to think that I was. But my personal items, scattered across a small table and on the polished hardwood floor, gave assurance of reality.

As I sat in the bed for a while, wrapped in crisp white sheets, I realized that the night before must also have been real—all of it, even the interaction with the small black and white photograph and the conversation and music it evoked in my head. Realizing I had spent the night in the home of Mrs. Camille Cunningham Sharp, and remembering the people in the photograph, I was left with a resolve to do my best to embody their dreams. I wanted to use my life to ensure a better one for others. I fully understand the value of being visible to all.

In spite of the lessons of race and place that had come alive at Roselawn Plantation, I felt energized. I felt I had the blessings of the fieldworkers to go about my business at the college and to represent them well. I got out of the tall bed and into the bathroom where I quickly got ready to start my day. Fully dressed, necktie and all, and with my shoes polished (one of my other holdovers from the military), I was ready.

I still felt a little awkward being a black male in the house with only white females, and I didn't know what the breakfast plan was. At that juncture, a butler would have been a welcome sight—but I still had not seen the black help. However, as I was getting my stuff together, I could hear faint sounds outside my door. I made them out to be the soft whirring of a vacuum cleaner. I thought I could also hear dishes clinking together. It was a weekday, and I knew what to expect. *Now the black servants.* I was prepared to meet the maid, the cook and whoever else who worked for Miss Camille. It was about time, even though I was prepared for the meeting to be awkward.

I quickly made one more trip to the bathroom to be absolutely sure I had not left a mess. I think I was obsessed with making sure that I was a good houseguest. Assured that my room was in order, I made my way to the door. Now I could clearly hear the sound of a vacuum cleaner somewhere close to my room.

The black help at last.

I envisioned the uniformed black maid who would have been pushing it. I didn't want to run into her. My plan was to get out of the room before the maid and the vacuum cleaner got to my door. I wasn't quick enough. When I opened the door, both the vacuum cleaner and the black maid were right in front of me. We almost collided. We both looked surprised, myself more than her.

The black maid was not at all what Little Cliff had expected. She was pushing the vacuum cleaner, but she was fashionably dressed and not wearing a uniform. This was Miss Camille's world, and I was finding it to be different in so many ways. Her maid was definitely not the stone-faced usher at the Governor's Mansion in Jackson, Mississippi. Taking in her demeanor and her dress, all I could hear in my mind was Aretha Franklin belting out *R-e-s-p-e-c-t! Find out what it means to me.*

Now there we were, two black people facing each other in the hallway at Roselawn Plantation. I think we both laughed out loud. What else could we do? Even though we had never met, I knew that we had grown up on similar paths. It didn't matter that I was an author and the guest at the home she cleaned. I knew her story and she would know mine. I had seen her a thousand times. She was my mother, my sisters, my aunts, and my female cousins.

While I was taking everything in, she gracefully moved back from the door to give me space to slide past the vacuum cleaner, and then she spoke right up. "Well, bless God, you must be the writer," she said.

I was startled that she knew about me. I managed to get out, "Yes, ma'am, I am the writer."

"Well, it's nice to make your acquaintance. I'm Suzy Morrell. You here for long?"

"And I'm glad to meet you. Just one more night, and then back home."

Then she stepped over to the hall table and picked up a copy of *Once Upon a Time When We Were Colored* and asked for my signature. It was a gift to her from Miss Camille, she said. I signed the book and handed it back.

"Why, thank you kindly. I'm gonna read it, every single word of it. Now you go on back to the kitchen. Miss Camille's waiting on you."

"Is she up already?"

She gave me a look as if I had asked the most uncalled-for question in history. "Up already? Why, Honey, that woman turns on the sun."

I squeezed by, careful not to trip over the long electrical cord. She waited until I was out of the way, and then resumed her cleaning, humming under her breath. I wanted it to be *R-e-s-p-e-c-t.*

FOLLOWING THE SMELL OF coffee, I made my way to the kitchen, now prepared to meet the colored cook, now that I had met the colored maid.

In the hallway, I had passed again the photograph that had spoken to me so clearly the night before, and the overwhelming realization of just how invisible we had been came back. I wondered if Suzy Morrell had ever noticed the photograph and the bent figures in its background. Here we were, their figurative descendants, a black housekeeper and a black author under the same roof at the same time. I could visualize the ships of change slowly passing in the night.

Remarkably, in the morning sunlight, the small framed photograph seemed to be powerless. I felt no pulling at all. For all practical purposes, it was just one of many vintage photographs. Somehow, I understood that all I was to experience had already happened. The night's encounter had been set up for me. The next steps would be up to me. The picture and the posture of the people in its background were firmly planted in my head along with the late-night conversation it had generated within me. I would not forget that night and I would not forget that picture.

I walked on through the dining room, past the long formal dining table and the massive chandelier. I walked through the den that housed a television, the only noticeable concession to the twenty-first century, and on into the small breakfast room off the kitchen. As Suzy had promised, Miss Camille was waiting. She was alone. The food was out. There was no black cook.

Miss Camille rose immediately and we exchanged morning greetings. She stretched again on her tiptoes to give me a warm morning peck on the cheek. I told her I had met Suzy Morrell, to which Miss Camille just nodded knowingly and smiled.

She motioned me to sit and said, "Now, Mister Taulbert, it's just us. The two professors from New Hampshire left earlier. Their session starts fairly early, I was told."

"Miss Camille, do you know how I'll get to the college?"

"That's all taken care of. I'll be driving you," she replied.

I'll be driving you was ringing in my ears. Admiring Miss Camille's vitality and tenacity at her age was one thing, but to actually ride with her was a different prospect. I had experienced the driving habits of an aging white plantation owner before, Miss Spencer of Glen Allan, and I silently prayed Miss Camille would not be like her. My great-grandpa was always leery of

Miss Spencer's driving and often said, "That white woman drives like a bat out of hell. Stay clear of her, you hear me?" But that advice would do me no good this morning, and there was nothing left for me to say.

My place was already set with hot English muffins, homemade peach jelly, some fruit, juice, water, and coffee. And there we sat, the black writer and the white plantation owner, in a scene so different from that in the hallway photograph. Having breakfast together seemed natural to her, and it almost was for me, but not quite yet. I was still a guest because of an invitation I had yet to fully understand.

As I sat at the round wooden table, I could see through the windows the fields stretching out from the mansion in several directions—acres and acres that seemed to have no end. Off in the distance were large farm machines, moving slowly down the rows. But I could imagine with great clarity how those fields would have looked decades earlier, with dozens of stooped field hands toiling away at planting, chopping, or picking the cotton. I knew that world up close and personal. I did not know the view from the mansions that oftentimes anchored the fields where we worked. I was on the outside, where we had been for generations. The inside was for "them."

To move from "them and us" is still the journey most of us need to take. Even while sitting over breakfast with Miss Camille, as if our worlds had always been this way, I was painfully aware that far too few of us reach outside our comfort zones to include others at our tables. Miss Camille was obviously among that special few. She had extended this invitation to me in the twilight of her life. I could not help wanting to understand her motivation.

I didn't say anything to her as we sat together. We were separated by race, age, gender, and social standing, yet we were bound together by a conjoined history that had been part of our birthrights—a history often too painful and complicated to discuss. We chatted about everything else, but nothing was said or even hinted at regarding the chasm that still defined our worlds. Instead of conversation about the lingering issues of race and place, I focused on my butter and muffins. Miss Camille even offered to get me more food. That's when I finally figured out that she had prepared our breakfast herself.

I jokingly asked Miss Camille about grits, a Southern breakfast staple missing from our table this morning. She smiled knowingly and said, "Maybe tomorrow." At that we both laughed.

With my breakfast nearly over, I nervously inquired about getting to the college. "Miss Camille, well, it's getting about that time isn't it?"

"Now, Mister Taulbert, slow down and take your time. It'll take me no time at all to get you to the college. I know exactly where we have to go."

I could only be amused as the elderly planter set me straight. And there we were, sitting together, with both our pasts close by. Yet we talked and made plans for the rest of the day as if our worlds had never been divided.

With the last of our food eaten and the dishes put away in the sink, I waited in the den as Miss Camille walked up to the front of the house and spoke with Suzy Morrell, still the only black worker I had seen at Roselawn, though I, and especially Little Cliff, was still looking. I wasn't purposely listening, but I could hear Miss Camille and her housekeeper/maid bantering. I could not make out their conversation, but I did hear them laughing together, probably at me.

WITHIN MINUTES, MISS CAMILLE was back in the den, purse in hand and keys out. We were ready to start our day's journey. We carefully walked down the steep steps as she naturally held on to my arm. At the bottom of the steps, I looked back and there was Suzy, waving and watching us from the back veranda. I have no idea what her thoughts were as I was about to be whisked away by her employer to lecture at the college while she remained behind to do her chores. I still wanted to ask her if she had noticed the people in the background of that little photo, and, if so, how it made her feel. I wanted to ask how she viewed her job and her relationship with Miss Camille.

I hoped that her work as a maid was not as my mother's had been in Glen Allan. I had heard her accounts of how she was treated. But it was Mama's job, one she had to brace herself to endure each day. She had six children and was divorced. She needed the weekly twelve dollars.

I sensed that Suzy Morrell's humanity was not being trampled on. She was the black help, but unlike the maids I remembered. Instead of the timid waves my mother would give us from the back seat of her employers' car as she was being driven off to do her chores, Suzy's wave was robust and obviously meant for both of us, the guest and her employer. I still see that picture in my head of her, leaning over the veranda railing, smiling, waving broadly, and carefully watching over us. I imagined that once we were safely away, Suzy returned to her world of housework—a world where singing and humming a tune were ordinary and sometimes expected.

Recalling my days of fieldwork and my job at Mr. Hilton's store and all that I had observed over the years, I understood the power of melodies from the soul. Humming had gotten us through many days of drudgery and it looked as if it was doing the same for Suzy. I imagined her with vacuum cleaner in hand, humming her away through the "big house" where, despite outward appearances, time and history had not quite stood still.

R-e-s-p-e-c-t! Find out what it means to me.

12

Our Bridge to Cross

"He who cannot forgive breaks the bridge over which he himself must pass . . ." —George Herbert

THERE WAS A HOT MORNING BREEZE AS MISS CAMILLE AND I slowly made our way to the car. I may have been ready to leave, to make sure not to be late, but Miss Camille was taking her time. I let my mind wander back to my childhood, and of course to the previous night of thinking about the great divide between the races. I was still amazed at the sequence of invitations that had led me to Roselawn Plantation. The journey, though unexpected and unplanned on my end, was turning out to be more than I could have imagined.

Only the realization that I had a job to do brought my wandering mind back to my present reality. I was ready to get to the college and get things set up for the morning lecture. Without Miss Camille, I had no way to get there, and I soon realized that she was not merely taking her time but had actually stopped walking. Then I saw her son Don making his way across the grounds toward us. Don now ran the plantation. I didn't know him well, but we had briefly met and talked a bit on my earlier visit. I saw quickly now that my time was not important. So I resigned myself to let mother and son have their morning meeting.

Standing in the hot morning sun, surrounded by cotton fields and shadowed by a Low Country mansion, I could not help seeing Don in the context of that hallway photograph. Little Cliff was wide awake and fully aware of what this morning scene represented. Don was not a peer, but one of "them."

I had to wrestle with my thinking. This was the twenty-first century and some of the change that Sam Cooke wanted for all had come, even if much remained to be done, materially and emotionally. While I braced myself to embrace what was possible, I could not help but think how we had allowed color to define much of our existence. Even so, and even here, surrounded by the vestiges of the past, I could sense a new reality that would not have been possible forty years earlier.

I knew my thoughts, but I had little idea what might be on Don's mind and how he felt about me spending the night in his childhood home. We were not meeting in a public accommodations space where laws and legislation had helped to move black folks along as equal citizens. We were on private property, where private thinking and acting could easily run its course. I was hopeful, but I didn't know what to expect, especially with the picture of the stooped black fieldworkers seared in my brain.

As Don got closer, I could tell that he was in his work clothes—well-worn jeans and a comfortable plaid shirt. After all, it was a workday on the plantation. I had seen so many of those days while growing up. Don had on his work clothes, but his walk towards us was telling. He walked like an owner—knowing that wherever his foot touched, the land beneath it was his.

We weren't that far apart in age. In another world, we could have been friends when we were growing up, but not in the severely divided times into which we were born. I made up for some of that division while in the United States Air Force during the end of the Vietnam War. We young soldiers were forced to live beyond our cultural comfort zones, and because we did, friendships for life were formed that otherwise would not have happened. For me, being both a soldier and living outside the South was good. I wasn't sure if Don had been a soldier or had lived outside of the

South for any period of time. Don and I were born into the complicated Southern system of Jim Crow segregation. Perhaps his acculturation, over time, had taught him to embrace as natural the benefits of white privilege and to ignore the black lack of same. I just had to wait and see.

However, sharing breakfast with his mother and experiencing her graciousness were almost making me want to defy Little Cliff, throw caution to the wind and maybe capture the dream I had when I was in high school and our bus driver would tell us every day that we would soon be picking up white kids on our bus route (in my school years, that day never came).

I hadn't thought of him in decades, but it suddenly came back to me about the Thomas boy who lived down below the colored school in Glen Allan—a friendship missed. Mama Ponk always referred to him as the "white Thomas boy." He and I played cowboys and Indians. We were sharpshooters with our BB guns and could climb Aunt Mary Ann Peters's plum tree like bushy-tailed squirrels. Our laughter was genuine, but it eventually ended. As puberty began to kick in, our respective grown-ups put a stop to the budding friendship.

Don and I had long since passed puberty. Somehow in my mind, the separation "line" was still there despite the impact of time, the civil rights movement, and federal legislation. It should not have been that way, but it was. I had shared the table and conversations with notable people, but this morning, having sat with the likes of Martin Lee, the great Chinese caretaker of Democracy, didn't matter. Uneasiness was keeping me on guard. We weren't surrounded by tall buildings and great monuments. No, we were surrounded by cotton, the complicit partner in the system of slavery. I wasn't Don's high school buddy. My presence was all his mother's doing.

Miss Camille smiled widely at the sight of her son. And I could tell right off that he was glad to see his mother. I watched from a short distance as they affectionately greeted each other. It was no different than I would have done with my mother.

To my surprise, Don didn't wait on me to walk over and join them. Instead, he marched right over and extended his hand. I had no idea what Miss Camille might have told him. Of course, she might not have told him anything. It's just that his response to me was not in keeping with plantation surroundings. His handshake reminded me of his mother and her lack of hesitancy when we first met. I know that such a gracious act would not have happened to me while I was growing up. Still, Little Cliff was not quick to abandon caution. I shook hands with Don, but adopted an attitude of wait-and-see. Meanwhile, Don immediately dove into the conversation.

"Well, Clifton, you're all duded up this morning. You gotta be hot in all that stuff."

I wasn't expecting that, but he had tossed the ball to me and I had to run with it. "Yep, you're right; the heat and the humidity are getting to me, but this is my uniform for the day, tie and all."

"Better you than me."

We both laughed, me somewhat cautiously. I had to be sure that he was not just going along with his mother by being cordial to me for the moment. This is the nature of second-guessing such "right off the bat" camaraderie across the racial divide. The lingering lessons have taught me to look for body language that might be holding a different conversation. I sensed none of that. He seemed completely at ease with himself, and with me for that matter.

"Clifton, tell you what, got a few minutes? Why don't you join me on the tractor? I can give you a quick ride around the place and show you what we got."

It was a simple invitation, nothing fancy or make-believe, to join him in the air-conditioned cab of his tractor. I was not prepared for that down-to-earth response, but Don's early morning invitation meant more to me than an invitation to an NBA game. He was inviting me into his personal world of work. His mother's invitation had been an unexpected bombshell; his was just as surprising.

It was interesting that the invitation was to see what they had. I could sense the pride in his voice. He had grown up there and was probably emulating his father. Don had asked me to ride with him and see the full scope of the plantation that meant so much to him but had brought up so many memories for me—memories that were a far cry from his.

I wanted to be on that tractor. I wanted that tractor ride. Even though Little Cliff had reasons not to, the adult Clifton recognized an opportunity. Knowing the South as I did, I found this invitation to be redemptive in an unexpected sort of way. I was sure Don's invitation was genuine. He was striking me to have been raised to believe that you only say what you mean or nothing at all. I would have given anything to say, "Yes." I needed that opportunity of just being me, not viewed through the lens of race, but I had a schedule to keep.

Realizing I would not be able to take him up on his offer, we talked for several minutes longer while his mother stood intently watching us. It was so interesting to see her just standing out of the way of the men's conversation, as it were. Understanding that I could not accept his offer today, we shook hands—a firm handshake, I might add—and I took a rain check. Yeah, I took a rain check to ride in a tractor cab with a white planter. Don said goodbye to his mother and walked off, in a moment climbing easily up the steep steps to his ancestral home.

I was reflecting that to change the past that both Don and I knew would require intentionality on both our parts. At the same time, my head was not without song, a song from a period the both of us would have known well.

Like a bridge over troubled water, I will lay me down.

I felt as if Simon and Garfunkel were calling us to intentional action that morning. The song seemed to urge us to become the bridges that would straddle the history that shadowed our lives. The photograph that had held me captive the previous night clearly showed me what was missing and the troubled waters that lay between us. Beyond Roselawn, changing America for the better would require all of us to step up and, extending a firm handshake as Don did, take it further and extend an invitation.

REFLECTION TIME WAS OVER. I had work to do. It was time for Miss Camille to get me to the college. I made my way to the car and, as always, held the car door open for Miss Camille before walking around to the passenger side and settling in for the ride. At that moment, everything seemed all right. Deep inside of me I knew that what I was experiencing thus far was not ordinary. Little Cliff understood this even more, and I could feel his reluctance to hold a conversation suggesting "all was well." I didn't even want to tell Miss Camille about the memory of the "white Thomas boy" and how my morning encounter with her son had made me feel welcome and respected. Instead, I remained gracious, but cautious. I did let her know how disappointed I was in not being able to take Don up on his offer to take a tractor ride around their place.

Just as she had said we would, we made it to the college on time. We pulled up in a cloud of dust, but she didn't come in this time. She had errands to run in town—the post office and things to get from the general store for "the boys," her term for her son and the field help that I yet to meet. She patted me softly on the back of the hand. Each time she patted me like that it reminded me that back home, for the most part, white hands went out of their way to ensure that they didn't actually touch ours. I could still remember having to slide change along the counter while working at the Hilton Food Store to ensure my black hands didn't touch white hands. This was not an issue with all white people, but it was with enough to make me remember when it accidentally happened; I had to be prepared for it to cause problems each time.

Miss Camille was responding in the exact opposite manner and being intentional about it. Looking me in the eye, as she always did, she said goodbye. I stepped back as she put the car in gear and drove off. I stood on the sidewalk and watched a cloud of hot Allendale dust cover her trail. When her Cadillac was out of sight, I walked into the college lobby, where I was greeted by Little Camille and several of the college administrators I had gotten to know over the years, all unaware of the night I had just had and the morning that was still in my mind.

Little Camille was running around, talking and sounding deeply Southern, as only she could, taking care of everybody. Over the years, I had grown to appreciate the honesty and inclusivity of her caring, further helping me to understand that we can move beyond the past. Her actions allowed me to remain hopeful. I never hesitated to extend her a hand. So, with everybody pointed in the right directions, Little Camille turned to me and, always the hostess, was quick to point out that the conference room was stocked with "sweet things," as she called those bundled and packaged calories. I laughingly followed her finger and walked into the empty conference room.

I filled a paper cup with orange juice and managed to pass on the pastries as I made my way to my lecture room to prepare for my talk about the *Eight Habits of the Heart* as the principles to build good community and establish meaningful relationships. Meaningful relationships across racial lines were—and are— very important to me. I recognized their value and recall with clarity how the military had provided me that first opportunity. I was young then, and Little Cliff was more than cautious, but the intention of the military to build young men of diverse backgrounds into teams would give me a much-needed perspective on what could be.

I WATCHED AS MY room filled up. I knew what I wanted for each participant. I wanted the educators to embrace the power of their own intentionality and to see themselves as bridges over troubled water for the generation of young people under their watch. I wanted them to understand that they could be agents of change to create new and welcoming lessons beyond race.

Without referencing where I had just spent the night, I jumped into the lecture, determined to point out the value of community in all our lives. I had come to teach them. They had no idea what I was being taught. I was able to end the day more motivated than ever to help others understand how important we can all be in each other's lives. The workshop went well and ended with a reminder to all of us of what is possible if we choose to be the difference we want to see. With the workshop over earlier than planned, I sat in the lobby along with the other facilitators and waited for Miss Camille.

Just like clockwork, Miss Camille showed up when she had promised. At first I didn't see her because she had parked in a different place. However, her daughter saw her and in her usual manner, she nicely grabbed me by the arm and wordlessly pointed out front. Her face and expression said it all. Her mother was there to pick me up. I knew exactly what to do. I didn't want her mother to sit one minute longer than necessary in the hot sun. With my coat slung over my shoulder and my wheeled briefcase trailing behind, I said goodbye to my co-workers and made my way to her car.

Miss Camille was smiling as I opened the back door to put my stuff inside. To have a white plantation owner sit in the heat and wait on me was not supposed to happen, but she made it seem natural. It was as if she had been patiently waiting for me for years and I had finally shown up. And to think, it all started with several ladies tracking me down in a Philadelphia Hotel lobby. Maybe the paths of the black writer and the white plantation owner were destined to cross. For sure, I was not her son, Don, nor her grandson, Carl, nor even Alan, her son-in-law. I was unsure who I had become to her.

"Mister Taulbert, throw that box of parts in the back seat and tell me how your day went. I'm sure it went just fine."

I smiled and I told her the day had been good. The day *had* been good, but my smile was for her. *She valued my day.*

As we rode along the county road toward the turnoff to Roselawn, we talked some more about the seminar and somehow got into discussing a trip she had taken to Europe. "Mister Taulbert, I enjoyed all that I saw, but I was so glad to get back home. I'll show you some of the pictures we took while over there. But, I just love the South."

I understood missing home. I too had traveled throughout Europe and admired all that I saw, but my heart was never really captivated. I was always delighted to come home to my family and friends. Maybe that is what she meant when she said *I just love the South,* but I wondered. Did I love the same South? Obviously, my South would have included the lessons of race and place I had to learn and live by, now become some sort of albatross around my neck. But my family, Southerners all—I loved them. They made the humidity bearable and discrimination not so pervasive. They had kept racism out of our homes and off of our front porches. I wanted to say what I was thinking, but I didn't, and neither did Miss Camille.

It was quiet except for the purring of the well-kept car, until Miss Camille spoke up. "Mister Taulbert, after you get some rest, I want you to come with me to visit an old friend, someone I want you to meet and know."

"Sure, that'll be fine." Of course, I said yes, with no idea as to who this friend might be. After all, Miss Camille had turned out not to be a retired schoolteacher living in a red brick ranch-style home. Besides she was my hostess, and I couldn't say no. With that settled, I watched the countryside whiz by as she drove us home.

We finally made it to Roselawn—which once more jolted me into the reality I had not forgotten. How, Little Cliff wondered, had I ended up on the white side of town? As usual, I helped her out of the Cadillac, and together we made our way up the tall steps that had been so foreboding when I first saw them. Once into the kitchen, she let go of my arm and I gave her the box of mechanical parts that I had carried in. She picked up her rather large two-way radio off the kitchen table to contact her son. I can still hear her going through a series of "over and out" responses and asking

Don to "come in." His voice finally did come in, and she seemed relieved.

I headed to my room. As I walked through the small hallway, those invisible people forever bent to their labors didn't reach out to me as they had the night before. There was no need; I had heard the message from the photograph and it would not be forgotten. I walked on to my quarters, which still amazed me. Was this really where I was sleeping? I felt as if I had slipped in when no one was looking; being left out or refused entry becomes a way of life and is not so easily forgotten. On the other hand, I felt as though Miss Camille had removed the "Whites only" sign and was showing me that it was possible to change, even at her age.

I rested a bit and then made ready for our visit with her old friend. I tried to picture this friend. I had no clue who we would visit, so I found myself thinking of all the bigger-than-life things that had happened to me—things that definitely say "the black kid done well."

Maybe I felt the need to impress her friend, so that he or she would not stumble over my race. For instance, I had spoken before members of the United States Supreme Court. Surely this would set me apart. I am not quite sure if it was Little Cliff or the adult me trying to fix it just right and make my presence acceptable.

Miss Camille was waiting on the back veranda. Once in the car, I expected her to give me some history on the person we would be visiting. No, she simply started the engine and we were on our way. She never once mentioned the person we would eventually see . . . this Southerner whom she called an old friend and felt that I needed to know.

13

A Familiar Place

"A man travels the world over in search of what he needs and returns home to find it." — *George Moore,* The Brook Kerith

WE SAID NOTHING AS WE DROVE FROM THE HOUSE ON THE well-worn, dirt-packed road—lined with trees draped with Spanish moss—that figuratively led from the late nineteenth century into the twenty-first, in the form of the paved county highway beyond Roselawn. Miss Camille had not turned on the radio, but I was not without music. I situated myself for a long ride. All along the way, I was seeing evidence of the Mississippi Delta I had left behind. I recalled how, while growing up, I desperately wanted my life to be different than what I was experiencing day in and day out. Little Cliff understood and brought to my consciousness the soulful sound of Otis Redding.

Sittin' on the dock of the bay, watching the tide roll away . . .

I could picture Redding singing to all who dreamed of a different place in life. However, my bay was a cotton field with its long rows where I used to stand and look as far away as I could, trying to see something different. As a teenager, I felt a sense of expectancy as I intended to leave the fields of the Delta behind, along with the lessons of race and place that sought to define me.

I could sense Little Cliff's presence in Miss Camille's car as she drove us to a place that was familiar to her, but unknown to me. I was both comfortable and uneasy; the past had done such a far-reaching job in crafting the social constructs that defined both my and Miss Camille's lives that I found it difficult to be fully at ease.

This was a conversation I wished to have held with her. Her age would have provided the perfect first-person historical narrative. However, her age also called for restraint. I yielded to being respectful, placed the issues of race aside, and gave in to talking more about my trips abroad, about the lecture tours that had taken me to Germany, Central America, Japan, and Belgium. Telling her about those trips was relatively easy, and she was keenly interested and asked poignant questions. There were no racial minefields to consider in such a conversation.

Europe was the topic, but more about her life was the conversation I really wanted. I wanted to know about her life in the South and her views on race. Maybe that would give me some clue as to whom we had become for each other. Instead, I stayed in a conversational safe zone, and she just kept driving farther away from Roselawn. Finally, though, maybe sensing my apprehension, she did open up about this friend.

"Mister Taulbert, we'll be there in no time. We've always lived pretty close to each other down here," she said. "I've known him all my life and just felt I needed to have him know you. You'll really like him."

She reached over and gave me that Miss Camille pat on the hand. I call it the "grandma" pat—the one that says no matter what is going on, you are going to be all right. At least now I knew the friend was a man, but who was he? As she talked about this man, I did notice that she had become rather quiet and focused.

"He's older, now, and can't get around as he once did. He had an accident—a bad one—one that should never have happened. Oh, he had such a bright future, but I guess it wasn't meant to be. Things like that I'll never understand. But I know that the two of you will get along just fine."

I noticed that she had one of my books in the car, maybe to give him, whoever "him" turned out to be. I just knew that she knew everybody as well as their people and their people's people. This, too, is a Southern thing. She didn't say anything more. But I could see the sadness in her eyes. We were both quiet now, and the view continued to look more and more like Mississippi with its small wood-frame homes, all looking quite similar. In the Delta, such small homes were always part of the plantation system, and, just when you least expected it, a white-pillared mansion would appear around the bend. I anticipated that such a home would appear at any minute.

None did.

Then she was slowing down, signaling that we must be getting close to the destination. Now I realized that I had to recalibrate my thinking. I had been way off track. Without Miss Camille telling me, I knew exactly where we were. I was at my childhood home. We were in a black neighborhood. Miss Camille's old friend would be a black man. I was amazed, though I said nothing. No matter what her presence had evoked in my head years earlier when we first met, her actions were continually being the conversations I wanted to hear—they were her first-person account of race and place.

Finally, she nosed the long Cadillac onto a small dirt drive that led to a neat little wood-frame house. I just sat quietly, caught off guard. For once, Little Cliff was quiet, too. She switched off the engine, turned and looked at me with a bit of a twinkle in her eyes, and simply said, "We are here."

We had been holding conversations for several years, but her words were almost always limited. I expected much more than *We are here*. I honestly didn't know what to say as I got out of the car and came around quickly to open her door. This was not a place I had expected to visit with the plantation owner. By now my head was examining other incidents that were not as I expected them to be.

The list was getting longer, and none of it made sense to me based on the lessons of my past. Putting me in her guest quarters made no sense. Holding on to my arm whenever and wherever we were together made no sense. Driving me to the college each morning made no sense . . . and now *this*. On the other hand, each incident made all the sense in the world. The invitations she extended were ones that *should* have been extended, and I had no reason not to lend her the support of my arm. This is what people do for each other. This is the *inside* of the community that I had gone all over the world talking about.

She just smiled and patted me on the back of my hand, as she always did, and said not one word. This was the meeting of the mansion and the shotgun house. You had to have been with me to fully grasp the impact of what I was seeing. This is the ending you write, hoping that someone will take note and embrace the opportunity. But this was not the last page of a novel. This was her reality—one that she was bringing into my life.

I followed as she walked a small path that was obviously familiar to her—a well-worn dirt walkway that the hot South Carolina sun had baked into a sort of natural concrete. She made no missteps. Being taller than she, I had to duck my head several times to avoid overhanging limbs.

I suddenly thought about one of my favorite movies, *Driving Miss Daisy*. It just popped into my head, reminding me of the one thing I didn't like about the movie. I could not understand why Hoke's home and his life were never shown, as if they were of no importance. We never knew the way to his house or experienced the family that shaped his thinking and behavior. It was simply inferred. This one-dimensional look at black life has always bothered me, as if the pictures on our walls don't matter and the smells from our kitchens are of less value. Life matters! All life matters!

What could have such a successful movie as *Driving Miss Daisy* ignited had the moviegoers also gone to Hoke's house and sat at his table and embraced his people? This, however, was as if she was taking me to Hoke's house as she led me onto the front porch of a home she seemed to know well.

MISS CAMILLE KNOCKED ON the door. Of course, I was still too surprised to say anything. Being at that house and knocking on that door was not what I expected at all. No one immediately came to the door, so while we waited, she started to talk, sharing a bit more information about the black man she had simply referred to as an "old friend."

"Mister Taulbert, Willie Lee Morrell is such a good person. I've known him his entire life. I always stop in to check on him. When I heard your first talk and read your book, Willie Lee immediately came to mind as someone I wanted you to meet and, of course, him to meet you."

Who is this man? With this being rural Allendale County, how did they manage to strike up a friendship that has defied time?

I could hardly wait to see who lived behind that door. Being a Southerner myself, so much was going through my head. I knew he would be black, but how black? Was he partially white? The South is complicated, and color is a great part of that complication. I had no answers. I would have to wait and see who lived behind the door. To her comment, I just nodded my head as she knocked again:

"Don't worry, he's at home; can't get out much. A car fell on him when he was a young man. It changed the course of his life. It should never have happened. Oh, he was onto a brilliant future at the college until that awful accident. But he'll be so glad I brought you over to see him. I'm so glad you took the time." She said all this with sadness.

"No, Miss Camille, I'm glad you brought me," I answered as she knocked a bit louder. I *was* glad she'd brought me. I wanted to see this man. I was glad that she thought it important for two black men to meet. I felt ashamed about my earlier supposition that her use of "old friend" had immediately set me picturing someone white and important. Well, her old friend was important, yes, but not white. Little Cliff was wrong. I was not being taken to the home of one of her white friends to be shown off like an exceptional trophy.

Finally, I heard footsteps dragging their way to the door.

What is his relationship to Roselawn? Is he tall? Will he be big? I sure hope he knows that I'm black.

The knob turned and then the door opened, not wide, but enough for me to see his face. It was weathered and black. He looked like me, though his disability had made him look older than he was. He was reasonably tall and somewhat thin. The aluminum walker that had made the dragging sound was in front of him, not only helping him get to the door, but also keeping him from falling.

"Y'all come on in this house." He may have been housebound, but his voice was robust and inviting as he moved a bit to give us space to get around him and the walker. I had no apprehensions at being there. Our history was intricately linked, and I felt as if I were coming home to a place similar to the one that had first welcomed me into the world. His humble abode was no Roselawn.

Although I was elated to be in his home, I was still surprised at how it had happened. I was not visiting him because I had received a note from back home to visit someone who may not have been kin, but was close enough for a visit. That would have been expected of me. However, this visit was unusual.

This is not to say that blacks and whites didn't know where each other lived. Back home in my small neighborhood, whites came through all the time, not to visit with friends, but to pick up the help. That was my normal. This is what Little Cliff remembered.

Mr. Morrell backed further into his front room, talking all the while. "Now, Miss Camille . . . now who's this with you?"

He wasn't at all surprised to see Miss Camille. But he had to ask about me. I was the stranger. I was the surprise. The two of them were at ease. Miss Camille had led the way through the opened screen door without hesitation, talking to her friend as we stepped inside his modest home. I closed the door behind me and welcomed the coolness from his window unit. I was in very familiar surroundings. Even Little Cliff was happy here—Miss Camille had brought us home.

"Willie Lee, I brought over a friend, Mister Taulbert. He's here from Oklahoma. My daughter, Little Camille, met him in Philadelphia and invited him here to talk at the college. Now never mind that she heard him up North—he's a Southerner just like us. He was born in Mississippi. I first heard him talk at the college several years ago. I thought about you then. I knew I wanted the two of you to meet."

I spoke up, "Sir, I am glad to meet you. Miss Camille had me really uptight as I tried to imagine this old friend of hers, but I am glad it is you."

Mr. Willie Lee, almost in slow motion, lifted his weathered black hand from the walker and gradually reached out to me connecting our shared lives. I eagerly reached out and shook the hand he extended. We both smiled. He knew I was at home.

Mr. Willie Lee looked so familiar. Everything about him spoke of the working colored men from back home in Glen Allan, even the clothes he was wearing. Although he was virtually housebound, his smile lit up the small room and caused his face to wrinkle around the eyes. It too looked familiar.

Miss Camille continued her introduction.

"Now, Mister Taulbert, Willie Lee grew up around Roselawn. You've met his sister-in-law, Suzy, at the house this morning. We all had high hopes for Willie, but as you can see, that accident cut them short."

I saw the sad look in his eyes when she referred to the accident. I wanted to know more about what had happened, but no one was extending me any more information than what had already been said. They knew the story, but felt no need to go into details on my behalf. However, as quickly as a shadow passes us by, his smile came back as his conversation pulled us farther and farther into his home.

"Y'all come on in from the heat. Miss Camille, you all right?" he asked, looking her directly in the eyes. I could tell he genuinely wanted to know. I wanted to know why he cared so much. But no one was talking. I may have been a Southerner like them, but I was not a Southerner from Allendale. I was not privy to the details. I didn't know the back-story. I wasn't sure that such an encounter would have taken place during the time I grew up.

"I'm fine, Willie Lee, and you are looking better yourself," Miss Camille replied.

MAYBE I REMINDED HER of who Willie Lee Morrell might have become had he not suffered a tragic accident. In that brief moment, she had bundled all three of us together as Southerners. Mr. Willie Lee seemed not to care one bit. Maybe he had heard her say this before. But I, on the other hand, was well aware of at least two Souths in the same room—the South of Roselawn Plantation and the South Mr. Willie Lee and I both shared.

As they talked between themselves, I was busy taking inventory of all that I saw and felt. The South I remembered was all around me as I named the various smells that came my way. Inside his humble home, ointments, liniments, cooked food, and even a hint of Old Spice welcomed me. I knew all those smells. I was immediately comfortable and at ease. Unlike at Melrose, I knew that I was welcome at the start. There was no reason for me to second-guess myself. In this home, I could throw caution to the wind. Except for a few minor differences, I might as well have been in my great-aunt's home where I was raised.

As I sat in this rather unusual company, I watched their every move. I listened closely to every word. I could hear caring. I could sense something beyond what I would have expected. It was quite a moment! As inclusive as we were for that moment, I still found it interesting that he called her "Miss Camille." At first, I wanted to say to myself, *see, nothing has changed. Respect is not being equally shared.* However, I thought for a moment and realized his age, not too different than mine, would have dictated respect for the older lady. He had been raised the same as me. On the other hand,

Miss Camille introduced me as "Mister Taulbert." That afternoon so many of the lessons of race and place I knew so well were being ignored. None of the typical social protocol really mattered. Their conversation was one of caring between two people who lived in close proximity, but were also worlds apart.

Life is complicated everywhere, and nowhere more so than in my South. Had the two educators from New Hampshire been with us, I doubt they could have picked up on the nuances that spoke volumes about how these two people had come to care for each other. Of course, it wasn't the integration I was promised, but it was way ahead of what I had witnessed as a child. I understood those critical nuances of tone and gestures. I knew that world. I know what I felt emanating from them as they talked. In that small front room, unencumbered by the outside world where racial division still mattered to so many, I could sense an honest community in the making. In Mr. Willie Lee's front room, it seemed as if both Camille Cunningham Sharp and Willie Morrell had, on some accommodating level, thrown caution to the wind. In that humble setting and for that short period of time, Little Cliff, the keeper of my memories, was at peace. He was witnessing race and place taking a back seat to care and concern.

I stood in the midst of their accommodating relationship, not fully understanding how it developed and why it had lasted so long. It was indeed strange to see the small-statured white planter standing beside this broken-down black man, each honestly inquiring about the health of the other. This is what I should have witnessed while growing up, but it was better late than never.

Mr. Willie Lee, being a Southern gentleman, stood back as we made our way to his seating area around a simple mantled fireplace. There we were: the plantation owner, the writer, and the disabled man. We were somewhere in the future and somewhere in the past. Although he had moved around to make space for us, he nevertheless continued his conversation with his friend who had said that he was looking better, to which he replied in a conversational style I easily recalled.

"Feeling better, I sure am. I'm so thankful, so thankful; mighty thankful. Come on 'round and y'all take a seat, make yourself to home. It's a little close in here, but we can make room. Yes, sir, we always make room at this house." He sort of laughed. This was his castle. He knew I had seen Roselawn and that his home was not the Big House. It didn't seem to bother him—the disparity that was obvious on so many levels. He was glad we had come to his small abode. The room was definitely crowded with his life. Just like Mama Ponk's house. He had his personal stuff within easy reach. Multiple boxes were in the corners—keepsake stuff, I assumed. It was all there, the furniture I remembered, and the simple straight-backed chairs. There were no chintz and brocade floral patterns anywhere to be seen. There were no antiques and there were no framed photographs lit by soft yellow lights. It was simply the home of this other Southerner who lived down the road apiece from Roselawn.

I laughed inwardly as I imagined the multiple purposes of his small front room, from sleeping to eating to entertaining your very best friends. *What a great room!* My soul was at ease. I could easily pat my foot and hum a tune. I was at home.

I was so taken with all the familiarity I was experiencing that I almost missed the charm of his extended welcome. He had offered us a seat, but Little Cliff noticed that Miss Camille stood. I wondered for a moment if she had ever taken a seat for her visits. The thought just crossed my mind; I guess I will never know. But I took a seat, and quickly. I had received such invitations all my life from the people back home, and grabbing up a chair was expected. So I did. Assured that we were both somewhat comfortable, he and his walker slowly made their way to the other side of the room, the side approaching a small hall-like turn that led further back into the house—another bedroom no doubt—and, of course, the kitchen. He slowly and carefully backed up to a chair that accommodated him.

I looked and listened for others in the house, but it was just the three of us. After all, it was a workday. So as he and Miss Camille kept visiting, I looked around at all that was tacked and hung on his walls: calendars, pictures—framed and unframed—and old news clippings. It was so familiar that I could imagine that at any moment Mama Ponk would come from the kitchen with a plate of fried chicken wings and rice cooked in rainwater. I took in all that surrounded me, completely comfortable, while Miss Camille kept the conversation going. I observed that she was now alternating between Mister Taulbert and Clifton when referencing me.

"Clifton, Willie Lee ran into some awful bad luck, but he's a survivor. And when I first heard you talk about your people in the Delta and how they rallied around your life, I could not help but think of Willie Lee. I just wanted y'all to get to know each other."

Despite all that South Carolina had yet to do to improve race relations in a place that had been so sharply divided for centuries, I sensed that the two of them had carved out a place to accommodate their friendship. It had to be complicated—they came from two highly structured different worlds—but I was observing a breakdown in that historical structure, a breakdown that is essential to building new and inclusive ones. The structures put in place to define their worlds were created long ago and had acquired a sense of permanence. In some small way that hot afternoon, we were all defying the past—the world that Little Cliff knew all too well. I took in everything as I watched and listened to them speaking words of genuine concern for each other. His family's connection with Roselawn must have run deep, and the connection seemed to be of value to the both of them.

Miss Camille told him everything about me: my travels, my books, and even some of my awards. I think she was letting him know that she had checked me out before bringing me into his life. She respected him and found it meaningful to share my success with him, which also highlighted her respect for him. On the other hand, it was obvious that Miss Camille's words carried weight with him. He listened and took in all the accolades she accorded me. (She had remembered nearly all of them. I was surprised once again.)

Even so, I could tell that Mr. Willie Lee was doing his own vetting and in his own way. I could see him making his assessment—shaking his head and looking across at me and then back to Miss Camille and shaking his head some more. He heard Miss Camille, but he was drawing his own conclusions about this familiar stranger sitting in his front room. I had seen that type of deep looking before. It was so typical in our small "colored" communities. His eyes were looking into mine to get a good sense of who I was. This was commonplace when I was growing up. The elders in our communities were soul-searchers who knew how to ferret the good characters from the bad.

While we were in the conversation about my travels and the good fortune my life had encountered, Miss Camille quietly passed her copy of my book to me. "Mister Taulbert, I want you to autograph this precious book to Willie Lee. Willie Lee, you are going to enjoy every page. I sure did."

We all smiled at her praise. After signing it to "Willie Lee Morrell," I handed him *Once Upon a Time When We Were Colored*. It was indeed his story as much as it was mine. The exchange was as meaningful to me as the day I pressed one of my books into the hands of Supreme Court Justice Sandra Day O'Connor. Mr. Willie Lee held it close to his shirt. I guess out of courtesy, he waited until he was sure that Miss Camille had finished her talk before he spoke up. But when he did talk, it was all so familiar.

"So, Mr. Taulbert—am I calling it right?" he politely asked, as he looked me directly in the face.

"Yes, sir, you are, but please call me Clifton," I said as I turned to face him and look in his eyes. "Oh, all right, Clifton, it is. So you wrote this book. You know this is my first time to visit with a real live author. I'll hold on to this book. Now is this your first time to South Carolina?"

Sort of laughing, I answered him. "Oh, no, no, no way, sir, I've been coming here for several years now." I looked over at Miss Camille, who was smiling.

"Good, good, that's good," he said. "Yes, yes, I got your book right here and thank you kindly for signing it. You got good penmanship. Miss Camille is still interested in my learning, even though the accident changed everything. I could have been a professor by now. They all said I had it in me."

I remember the flicker of lost hope in his eyes as he quietly mentioned a life that he had dreamed but never knew, back to his youth, I suppose, when he was filled with vitality and those around him, including Miss Camille, saw a bright and promising future. I glanced at Miss Camille. She was quiet and thoughtful as well. For a brief moment, we all paid homage to what could have been.

"You would have made a great professor," I said. "It's all in your eyes. They sparkle when you talk."

Miss Camille just stood off to the side, letting us talk for a while; nothing serious, just talk about my work, my travels, and my family back in Mississippi. I could tell by the way he held my book that he was pleased to have it.

Just at the right moment, Miss Camille spoke up, and I listened. I sat on the sidelines of their conversation. It was obvious as they talked that he really had been headed to college and really had had a bright future. I sensed he really would have made a great professor.

I'll never know the depth of the relationship between them, or how and why it continued through all the racial turmoil South Carolina had seen and across a color divide that was almost etched in stone. I was suddenly struck by the realization of how laws and customs had been used to chisel that stone in formal and informal ways. What was the N-word, the N-jokes, except a tool used to shape our differences in ways that benefited the few at the expense of the many. And here sitting before me were two models of the extremes of the South that had resulted. Yet I can only bear witness to what I saw and what I felt transpiring in front of me. In that room that afternoon, I saw that the N-word was way off in the distance—a word not used in a world where people cared for each other. From where I sat in Willie Lee's straight-backed wooden chair, I saw genuineness that had little or nothing to do with the homes these two people lived in or the worlds that surrounded them, the colors of their skins, or the histories of their respective journeys. They conversed at a different level. Both were too old to pretend, and there was no need to do so for my benefit. My eyes were taking it all in, with hope for our shared future bubbling up inside of me as I watched them.

I could hear the lyrics from the Hollies: *He ain't heavy, he's my brother. His welfare is my concern.*

We had thrown caution to the wind and for a brief interlude recognized and appreciated how valuable we were to each other. I hummed under my breath as they talked. Somewhere in that complicated Southern relationship between the plantation owner and the crippled worker were promising possibilities for the future for all of us. Moving beyond the past is not always easy, but it is possible.

It's a long, long road from which there is no return, while we're on the way to there, why not share?

That afternoon, again in an unexpected place, those lyrics could have been the voice of one of my elders from back home when I was still a young boy, wrapped in winter clothes, holding tightly to my great-aunt's hand. It could have been Miss Josephine Stanley who, knowing of the sickness of my great-grandmother, stepped out of her small house and hollered across the road to me and Mama Ponk as we made our way to sit with Mama Pearl.

If you need me, call me. I'll be home.

Miss Josephine's words are forever etched in my consciousness. Other people matter. We can all share. Our humanity is not determined by the physical assets of our lives, but simply by the gift of life. It's all right to "be home" for each other.

In the comfort of Willie Lee Morrell's cozy front room, I sat and listened as two friends talked about a world that was familiar to them, hearing all the while the meaningful lyrics and words in my head.

My being there was indeed an unexpected pleasure, but not one to last forever. We all had things to do and it was time to go. Miss Camille assured him that she'd be back, and it was obvious that she would be. Of course, Willie Lee extended an invitation to me to do likewise. I promised I'd stop by if ever again in Allendale.

He slowly and carefully rose from the chair, and—with great dignity, I might add—stood and clutched the arms of his aluminum walker. He led us to the door, safely making his way past boxes and chairs. With one hand holding the walker steady, he opened the wood door, then pushed the screen door open with the walker and stood in the open doorway as we walked past him onto the front porch. I shook his hand again and thanked him for his hospitality.

Miss Camille said, "Willie Lee, now you do what they tell you. Take care of yourself. Don't you worry, I'll be back."

"Now you do the same, Miss Camille. Mind your children. We ain't young no more," he laughed.

I WAS SMILING AS we walked away from his home and the world of a shared African American heritage I knew well. During that short visit with a man I had wrongly assumed would be of the white Southern aristocracy, I felt the same community that had permeated our small front room when I was growing up, so full of human warmth despite the Jim Crow laws that sought to reach into every aspect of our lives.

Community is not the place as much as it is the people and their actions within the place. Just like Mr. Willie Lee, there were those in Glen Allan whose life actions created the sense of community that I know to be power-ful and transformational. When I think of home, I think of people—their laughter, their unselfishness, their tears, and how they welcomed me to my life.

I had just experienced all that I believe in. I knew that our paths would probably never cross again, but that did not prohibit me from placing Willie Lee Morrell on my emotional mantle. His surroundings would indicate that he had missed out on much materially, but his spirit was strong and his appreciation for life was obvious. I had witnessed spirits like that all my life, people with so little of the world's treasures but filled with enduring habits of unselfishness. Such spirits nurtured my life while I was growing up and becoming a man in the midst of our legally segregated world. Without such people around me, I am certain that my life would have taken an entirely different course; hence my conversations around the world: build community and transform lives.

If Mr. Willie Lee was jealous or upset over the disparity between his life and that of his old friend, I couldn't sense it. The difference was obvious, but thinking back to my youth and my small cotton community, I don't recall being jealous of how white people lived, even when the differences were equally as obvious. When I first awakened to life on this planet, that's just the way it was. Did that mean it was the way it should have been or would always remain? Of course not. Sam Cooke's crooning reminded us of the *change* that was gonna come. So I do understand how Mr. Willie Lee would not have been envious of the material possessions of his friend Miss Camille, but I could feel that he was saddened over his lost opportunity to be his best.

Just as the framed photograph from the night before had evoked so much about the great divide, the reality I had experienced in Mr. Willie Lee's front room was painting a different picture of what could be possible. The divide is real, but so is our ability to bridge it, regardless of how long it might take. The outcome will be worth our efforts. And the generations of promise that surround us need to see what is required of them. Deep down inside I had always known this. There has to come a time in our lives when the mansion and the shotgun house no longer define our humanity.

Regardless of where he lived, I somehow sensed that Miss Camille's friend embraced that intangible gift of good community, just by being a caring person unafraid to reach out and welcome others. Their unique relationship may have happened over time. Or maybe it had always been that way; if so, what a testament to the goodness within us! I didn't ask. I just carefully observed. I could tell from the light in his eyes as we spoke that afternoon that he welcomed me and that my success had become his own. Yes, I had held the pen or struck the keys that wrote the books, but he beamed with pride as Miss Camille's copy of my book was pressed into his hand. I was an African American Southerner as he was. He knew my past and he celebrated my journey as if it had been his own. Miss Camille was right again: I needed to meet her friend. Yes, I signed a book that I had written for him, and, for me, he validated a conversation that I had heard all my life: other people do matter, and stuff and things should not be the essence of who we are. Upon leaving his "great room," I understood even more clearly the responsibility upon my shoulders to continue sharing the value and transformative power of community that I had also witnessed while a young boy growing up on the Mississippi Delta.

Though shadowed by my Jim Crow youth, I cannot afford to allow my life to be paralyzed or my voice silenced by those lingering lessons, no matter how long and invasive their reach. Perhaps my work is my destiny, helping to frame a new and enduring future, not just for myself, but also for the generations who would look to me. With my remaining time, I want to do my part, however small, to remodel our world as I pass through it. I owe this to the future as well as to those from my past who lived in servitude, dreaming of better, but unsure how "better" would look.

The visit to the plantation owner's old friend also seemed to have been orchestrated by destiny. Though hundreds of miles from the place of my birth, I was home among things familiar for an afternoon, witnessing a friendship that I would not have been able to imagine as a boy. Meeting Mr. Willie Lee was not what I expected, but he was just what I needed to experience. And now in the air-conditioned comfort of Miss Camille's black Cadillac, along with me, Little Cliff settled back to the quietness of the engine as we turned back toward the mansion that Miss Camille called her home.

14

Private Conversations

The words you choose to say something are just as important as the decision to speak. — Unknown

NEEDLESS TO SAY, DURING THE QUIET AND THOUGHTFUL RIDE from Mr. Willie Lee's home back to Miss Camille's world, I found myself filled with private thoughts and reflection—trying to further understand the complexity of our race relationships. The challenge and opportunity are great, especially among those of us who grew up in the Deep South during the time in which I did, because so much of that way of life has found its way into the present times although few want to see it.

When I was a child, the chasm between the races was reinforced with the lessons of race and place at every turn; thus their tenacious hold on many minds today. Growing up black was learning what one could not do and the consequences of doing the opposite. Growing up white was learning to accept white privilege and to fear giving it up. That whole afternoon with Miss Camille had been one where we were all doing the opposite of what we had learned. In Mr. Willie Lee's front room, for a brief moment in time, I was privileged to be present when caring hearts took the front seat.

I have often wondered what conversation might have been going through Miss Camille's head as she drove us home. After all, she was a daughter of the Old South and that day she provided me with a picture of how the New

South could look. I have often wondered how she felt about our visit and how it might have affected both her old friend and me. I had just witnessed the complexity of racial relationships being untangled, but I would have found it difficult to fully explain to someone who was not familiar with the challenging Southern culture the three of us shared. I saw two people, separated by race, gender, and status, but they nevertheless had deep concern for the health and welfare of each other.

Even though it was an afternoon clearly beyond my expectations, I still sensed that both had already established their new boundaries and knew just how far to push the social envelope. Great civility existed between them and was graciously extended to me, allowing me into their circle of friendship. I, too, knew just how far to go. It was more than I expected, but I dared not go further. Intuitively, I knew the boundaries. History made us all cautious.

Even so, Miss Camille continued to belie my expectations of what I would have associated with her rank and color. I felt as if our ride home should have been filled with conversation over all that had taken place. From my perspective, we had made history. I wanted to ask her about Mr. Willie Lee's folk and their historical relationship to Roselawn. I wanted to let her in on my expectation that her old friend would be white. Instead, I kept my feelings and all my conversations between me and Little Cliff.

She thanked me for going with her, and I thanked her for the opportunity. Nothing else was said. I guess I had become the student and it was being left to me to interpret all that I experienced. Maybe she knew that one day I'd write the book report on all that she had taught and all that we had learned.

Though I had come to my own resolution regarding my feelings of being in a familiar place while visiting with Miss Camille's friend, I could only speculate about their friendship and why it had continued for so long. I knew that Southern agrarian world so well. I know the courage it would have taken to toss caution to the wind and open your heart and your home to those who looked like me. We were the servants. Our color, for many, was simply the physical evidence of our enduring servitude.

I remember when I was right out of college and serving as the administrator for a retirement center in Tulsa, Oklahoma. One of our residents, a white lady, had retired to Tulsa from Alabama, where her husband had been a well-respected music teacher at Auburn University. It was so long ago, but I remember the incident and I can see her face as if it was yesterday.

Mrs. Avery Carnes was an older, heftier version of the actress Bette Davis. For her and all of the residents of University Retirement Community, it was my joy to serve their senior years as best I could, even though I was well aware of how some felt about my skin color. Day-in and day-out, I walked beyond the lingering lessons of race and place to do my best job possible as administrator of their home. One day, after she had been living there for many months, Miss Avery called my secretary to come to her cottage. At that visit, she confided in Barbara Clark that, despite all she had been taught about "colored" people, she thought surely that someone as nice as me must have a soul, after all.

As slavery increased and became a more permanent part of the Southern landscape, there were those who argued that black people were without souls, and thus white people were not accountable for their actions toward us. Such thinking, transferred from one generation to the next, negated the need to think of "brothers and sisters." Those without souls were destined to serve. That was that.

The residue of such thinking still exists, though it is not as pervasive as it once was. It shows up in many different ways. Not being valued as a human being with purpose is tantamount to not having a soul. Miss Avery was only one person, but I have a feeling that from her generation, she was not alone.

Before Mrs. Avery Carnes passed away, she gave me a small brown paper bag containing several antique silver spoons from her family, which we still have. She was finally able to call me friend.

The opportunity to reach beyond the past continues to stare us all in the face. It's possible to do so. Just get in a black Cadillac and keep driving till you get to your "Mr. Willie Lee's." Make sure you take a friend along.

WITH SOME TIME LEFT before I met friends for supper, I made my way back to the den where I sat with Miss Camille's dog, Summer, and watched the Weather Channel. I was prepared for rest and quiet relaxation. Instead, Miss Camille walked in and I learned that she had plans for us.

"Clifton, you've seen the log cabin on the property under the oaks? It's just across the way," she said while looking thoughtfully through the den window to the newly constructed log cabin that sat within a grove of oaks. Though modern, it, too, was surrounded by the past. Spanish moss was everywhere.

"Yes, ma'am, I have," I said.

"It's going to be my next and last residence."

"Your residence? Miss Camille, I thought your daughter was only teasing. I thought the cabin was your grandson Carl's, not yours." I couldn't imagine her giving up Roselawn for a log cabin, no matter how good it looked from the outside.

"Maybe one day it'll be his, but for now, it's being set up for my retirement years. I'm going to move out of this big rambling house. I've been here much too long. I want to walk you over there and let you see it."

There was nothing for me to do but stand up. I was on her agenda and the cabin was the next item. I would visit the cabin, and it was all settled. Even though I was prepared to join her, I had no idea what to expect. My visit to Mr. Willie Lee's house had shown me that. I just had to wait and see.

Within minutes, she was ready, heels and all. We weren't going to town, only a few feet into the grove of oak trees, but that was Miss Camille for you, still well dressed, totally defying the insufferable heat. We walked out to the back veranda where our routine continued. Taking my arm to walk down the steep stairs had now become commonplace. She reached out her hand and I extended my arm. With her walking maybe a half step ahead of me, I was careful to make sure that I did not misstep. I listened as she talked about the fields and their need for rain and what she hoped would be the end result of the boys' effort—a good crop. As we made our way down the steps, she talked about the plantation and past seasons when all of their work seemed to have been in vain. Seeds were planted, but no crops were forthcoming. She may have been somewhat tiny, but again, I could tell from her words that her actions defied her stature. When she talked, she grew taller, sturdy and determined—a determination she no doubt passed on to her planter son.

The sun was blistering, but she didn't seem to mind. The sun was essential for her cotton and was thus an ally and friend. Meanwhile, I was starting to sweat and to remember more than I cared to about cotton growing. As we walked from the back of the house across the open lawn, our reverie was interrupted by boisterous laughter coming from across the way, near one of the farm machine sheds. The building that had once been bright red was now weathered from the heat, the rain, and time. Intrigued, I slowed down and looked around. I saw several young black men sitting on a fallen or broken piece of farm equipment, shirts undone and their legs propped up, no doubt taking an afternoon break.

Well, some more black help.

I was finally getting to see the help that I had been looking out for since my first Roselawn visit. As we got closer to them and their laughter, I wondered how Miss Camille would respond. They weren't curly-headed blond Southern boys. They were sweaty, young, black fieldworkers. These were the young boys that, in some circles, white women were told to avoid at all costs, and, as I recalled from my youth, boys who upon seeing the plantation owner would have dispersed rather quickly.

If in urban America, Miss Camille and those like her would have been told to roll up their car windows and lock their doors and drive as fast as they could, putting distance between them and the trouble these young guys signaled. While I was assessing the situation, their familiar laughter took me back home to the Peru plantation. As a young boy, I would visit my Cousin Buster Lee and his family. His mother was my great-grandmother's sister, and Peru Plantation is where they lived. How the plantation came to be called "Peru" on the Mississippi Delta is not known. The boys I saw at Roselawn were about the ages of Buster's teenage sons, Earl and Jimmy Lee, who were always filled with laughter. I was hearing that same hard-farm-work laughter again. As we got closer to them, I was ready to see that other side of Miss Camille. After all, she was white, and the owner, and these guys were not writers—no books and lectures to their credit. I was prepared for some sort of social adjustment. I waited.

Miss Camille, without saying a word to me, simply dropped my arm, left me standing, and walked over to where the guys were. I watched as her tall heels made holes in the earth, and I watched as the young men stood up to greet, and, I assume, welcome her. I could see her waving her hand for them to sit back down. They did. That act, though normal and practical, amazed me. Buster's boys would never have been allowed to sit while a white person stood in their presence.

From the gestures I could see and the additional laughter I could hear, I recalled when I first met her and noticed how she knew the history of all the hands shaken and pats given. Would it be the same for these boys? From where I stood, I could make out that she knew each by name and family. As I said, I had earlier observed an Alex Haley-like quality in her. I heard the young men's respectful laughter and could sense the gist of a welcoming conversation. I knew these young men would be burdened with some of my lingering lessons of race and place, but I also knew that the weight for them would not be as heavy. Even so, I felt that they knew just how far to go, just as we knew how far to go when at Mr. Willie Lee's house. The past hangs on.

Miss Camille had surprised me once again. When she walked back over to where I was standing, she just took my arm, looked up, smiled, and resumed our walk to the log cabin. After all, she had extended to me the invitation to join her. I had become the student. It would be up to me to interpret what I witnessed.

She did share a bit of their conversation.

"Clifton, they are all good boys. I just keep telling them that they've got to stay in school. I'm sure they get tired of hearing me, but as you well know, they will need that extra education."

Later I would learn from Little Camille that they were also probably putting in their orders for Miss Camille's famous homemade hamburgers and South Carolina sweet tea that she served up in pint mayonnaise jars. The plantation owner was also a short-order cook. It was not Suzy Morrell's cooking that held them captive, but the hamburgers cooked up by the plantation owner. My childhood memories of multiple black cooks making those early morning journeys to the homes of their employers had so skewed my thinking that I found myself somewhat shocked that Miss Camille was actually a great cook herself.

We continued our walk into the grove of trees where a very modern twenty-first-century log cabin had come to life alongside a nineteenth-century plantation Low Country mansion. While still holding onto my arm, she began talking again as if I were family, or at least close enough, who needed to know her plans for her future. Keep in mind, I had not grown up in South Carolina, and, as far as I could tell, we had no immediate family ties, real or social. I could not help wondering who I was in her head. Why had she taken to me as if she had been expecting me to show up? We knew the social landscape of the world that had defined our roles. Yet I was welcomed as if that divide no longer existed. I could not imagine what she wanted to share with me or why. This was her cabin. This was all personal stuff, not usually information thrust upon a visiting author. I was not Carl, her grandson. She had other grandchildren, but Carl was the only one I had met. Still, none of that seemed to have mattered. As we got closer to the cabin, she was asking questions and talking as if my response mattered.

"Now, Clifton, do you like the outside?"

"It looks great to me."

"I wanted it to sort of fit in with the landscape."

"Well, it does, Miss Camille. It's really good-looking."

The cabin was rustic and the logs had yet to weather and change colors. It still looked brand new.

"Clifton, I do hope you like it."

"It's not like your other house. But I think I could stay here."

"I think I can, too. Do you think I am thinking right to prepare to move out of the other house?" She was looking into my face, asking all these questions as if my answers mattered.

"It's hard for me to say, Miss Camille. That's a big decision."

"It is, and I've made it. I can hardly wait to move in here and get settled. I'm so excited. Can't you tell?"

"Yes, Ma'am, it's all over your face."

"Unlike the old house over there, I was involved in every single detail of this design. The boy who designed it was a local builder, young and full of ideas, but I had ideas, as you can imagine. He soon figured that out. I wasn't building it for him, but for me. I wanted it just right, you know. You must see the inside."

She was beaming. She clearly enjoyed the fact that she had been successful as the general contractor.

"You know, Clifton, you have to think about the future. I didn't want to be sick or need care in that big house. It's nice, but it can be awfully inconvenient at times. I wanted something close to the ground and easily accessible for me and anybody else. I have no idea how long I can make my way up and down all those steps. Recently, I began to think that some carpenter slips in at night after I am sound asleep in the big house and adds one more layer of steps to my climb. Those steps are awful."

We both laughed.

"Plus, I wanted space for Summer to have good running room. Dogs need that, you know, even Miss Summer."

I DIDN'T FULLY UNDERSTAND her reasoning to leave Roselawn when a ramp could have been easily built to ensure ease of access. No matter, she had made up her mind and this new home would become her final dwelling place.

From the outside, the cabin looked as if it had walked out of an architectural magazine. It was nestled among the oaks, which provided a good-looking contrast of new, bright and shiny logs to trunks of the old trees. This lady had found a way to be in control of her life. I think she knew exactly what she was doing.

I just wish I was privy to more of her conversation about all the other acts of independent thinking and graciousness that she had afforded me. I had never expected our warm handshake in the college auditorium to evolve into anything else. Our first meeting left me confused and inquisitive—taking me mentally back to my segregated youth. And when I received the invitation to supper, saw her home, and learned her history, I realized why she had had such an impact on me. In the shadow of her Low Country mansion, Little Cliff and all he remembered from Glen Allan burst forth. Over time, as our paths continued to cross, it was as if our lives were meant to intersect and all that I had encountered was meant to have happened, even standing there with her on her cabin's front porch. I can't explain it, but I feel it was meant to be. As she released my arm and started rifling through her purse for the key, I knew that I was at the right place. I politely stood off to the side.

"Where is the key? We just have too much in these purses."

I think I nodded yes.

When she finally found the key and tried to open the door, I could tell she was experiencing a bit of trouble, so I stepped in and asked if I could help. Without any hesitation, she turned, smiled, and gladly handed me the key. Then she stood back and allowed me to open the door. With a quick twist of my wrist, the door opened. Being a Southern gentleman, I stood back so she could enter first.

I could see and smell the newness just waiting to be lived in. From what I understood, even Miss Camille's close friends had not seen the inside, only her family and the designer she called "the boy." I may have been the first outsider to experience her personal tour of what she called her retirement home. The inside of the cabin was welcoming, but it was not Roselawn. Except for a few vintage pictures that I could see as I quickly glanced around, she had intentionally left the nineteenth and twentieth centuries on the outside.

As we looked over the front room, she was careful to point out every little detail, and not just the design. She showed me the way it was laid out to handle a walker if need be, the lighting, and how the wall socket covers matched and blended into walls. This was not a spur of the moment decision. Miss Camille was living out a plan. And now I—the outsider in so many ways—was right in the middle of it.

It wasn't a large home, just big enough to be comfortable and not crowded with history as Roselawn was. She took me down the short center hallway, pointing out things here and there, before heading to the very back. I stood with her on the screened-in back porch where one day she said she would sit and watch the best of nature growing at her feet and her dog could run at will.

After sharing all she anticipated from her back porch, we started back into the main part of the cabin. This time, rather than pointing things out to me and moving on, she stopped. We were standing before two seemingly identical bedrooms, sitting side by side.

I couldn't begin to imagine why she wanted me to study these two unfurnished rooms. There were no pictures on the walls. There was nothing to see. That didn't matter; she walked me into the empty bedrooms and with her voice and hand gestures began to paint a picture about this place where she and a friend, a lady I had not yet met, would spend their last days together.

As she talked it was taking shape in my head. Pictures were hung on the walls. Pictures of family members were on nightstands. Bed coverings were in place and fresh-cut flowers in special vases were on corner tables. As she talked about how beautiful and accommodating these rooms would be, her voice changed and her laughter was replaced with a kindly seriousness I had not heard before. She talked and I listened. I still couldn't understand why she was telling all of this to me, but I listened and smiled, counting her friend lucky, whoever she was. I assumed it must be a distant relative, to have such nice retirement accommodations. While I was trying to understand where this conversation was going, her second conversation on race and place opened up.

"Clifton, my friend is black and we've planned this. We've planned to take care of each other."

I had not seen this coming. This was the same lady whom I had originally thought to be the reincarnation of Miss Jeffries from back home in Mississippi. This was the same lady whose "big house" had intimidated me, bringing to the surface moments in my life that I had wanted to leave buried. But she was also the same lady who took me to visit an old friend, Mr. Willie Lee, who I also had expected would be white. Over all the years that our paths had crossed, she had never referred to anyone by race or color, which would have been so common for someone from her era and mine as well. Our shared South was a world where "color" dictated and defined nearly everything and everyone. This instant was the very first time I had heard her refer to race at all. I had no doubt that she did this for me, not as a commentary, but as critical information I needed to know. She wanted me specifically to know that the friend who would have equal comfort was black. Had she been eavesdropping on my thoughts that day as we drove from Mr. Willie Lee's house? The inequity of place was on my mind that day. Yet Miss Camille had planned a future that challenged the past. She wanted me to know that.

I wanted to ask a thousand questions, but at that moment silence seemed best. There had been many times I wanted the subject of race and color to jump up so that we could hold that conversation. But no, in her reference to others, she would simply say, neighbor, friend, acquaintance, or son or daughter, or use their professional title. Not this time. This time, she specifically told me that the friend who would occupy the other bedroom was black.

She was looking me directly in the face when she told me. She didn't blink and neither did I. Yes, I was stunned. According to her, this friend was a lady she had known for years and they had made this agreement between themselves. She took the time to show me every single detail of both rooms and that both were outfitted equally. She especially wanted me to know this.

I never met the black lady who had agreed to intertwine her golden years with those of Miss Camille. I never had the chance to hear her side of the story. Yet, knowing Miss Camille as I was beginning to, and being constantly surprised, I could see how it was quite possible that somewhere in their respective Southern worlds, they had found common ground beyond race and place and had mutually agreed to be there for each other as their earthly days came to a close.

Of all that conversation in the new cabin, the words that stay with me are those about the comfort provided in both of the small rooms and how close they would be to the bathrooms.

"Clifton, everything will be identical. I've made sure of that. And see, look how close the bathrooms are to our rooms. It's going to work out just fine."

She took great pains to point out the bathrooms and how identical they would be without knowing how, when first at her home, I really had to use the bathroom, but my past was preventing me from asking. And while I was trying to deal with the call of nature, she had quietly come over and whispered in my ear the location of the bathroom. As she spoke, I thought of my earlier life where everything was separate and unequal. I am sure that it was even more so during her lifetime. Yet in these, her last days, she was somehow making sure that her life was not separate and unequal.

I wish you could have been in the room with me to witness the sense of "brotherhood and sisterhood" that existed in her log cabin. Sincerity abounded, and even Little Cliff recognized it.

There was really nothing for me to say as I tried to picture two older Southerners, one black and one white, sharing their last days together. I kept this new picture in my head. I will certainly not forget her conversation and the tenor of her voice as she talked. As we walked from the room, she gently patted me on the back of my hand, which had come to mean to me the extended conversation left for me to interpret. That was the immediate extent of our conversation. By now, I thought, we were ready to go, but not so. When we got to the small, intimate front room, instead of standing and talking, she invited me to sit down. She then pulled up her comfortable chair close to mine, again as if she had known me all her life. I could not help thinking of the small black and white photograph I had seen earlier and how it had held me captive as I saw the historical divide that once seemed so permanent. But it was not so this afternoon; and, for a while, the dividing chasm was gone. She was aging, but not hard of hearing. Yet, she chose to sit close by me. She leaned into my face and told me how she had carefully picked out the pictures I was seeing on the walls.

She pointed out several paintings. "My mother was quite a painter. She painted those pictures over there. I didn't want too much from the old house, but I wanted my mother here with me. She was so kind. She died early in my life, but I always think of her."

Her face lit up and she smiled widely as she talked about her mother, who must have been a good lady. Sitting privately with her in her future home, I now knew that the first unexpected touch I received from her in the college auditorium was the start of a journey that needed to be taken—one that I needed and that she needed to be a part of—two people recognizing the humanity of each other.

As our afternoon conversation was winding down, she looked into her purse and this time handed me the key. No conversation was needed; giving me the key seemed so natural. On the front porch, she stepped aside and watched as I locked the door to her future.

"It's shut tight, Miss Camille." I returned the key and watched as she dropped it into her purse.

Then, arm in my arm, we walked silently across the grass. I remember looking back at the tall oaks surrounding her cabin. The trees were plush with green leaves and the ever-present Spanish moss. It was an idyllic sight, and I thought it would be so even in the winter after all the leaves had fallen.

As we passed the machine shed, I looked up, and this time there was no laughter from young black men taking a break. However, way across the fields, I could see specks of red moving. The guys had gone back to work. I wondered what they had thought of me, the older black guy in the necktie. No matter. The farm machines were at work and so were the boys, her son, Don, included. They were farmers and were doing everything they could to ensure a good crop. I was a bit envious as I saw the big red machines slowly moving along the way. I could have been riding in the air-conditioned cab with Don and no doubt listening to country music. We could have joked and laughed. Maybe I could have taken my turn at driving. It could have been me and the "white Thomas boy," no longer separate and unequal.

THE INVITATION TO ALLENDALE at the turn of the century had turned out to be much more than an opportunity to speak at a college. It was looking more and more like destiny.

As we reached the steps of the plantation house, she looked up and smiled.

"Clifton, do you really like it?" she asked, as if my opinion mattered. I have no doubt that she genuinely wanted to hear my say on her log cabin.

Of course, it was nice. It was really state of the art, and I told her so.

"Bet you Abe Lincoln would have loved that cabin. It's really nice, Miss Camille, everything about it is nice, well thought out and planned. Are you sure, though that you can leave your beautiful home?"

"It won't be any trouble at all. I can leave this old house tomorrow," she answered. Her answer was not laced with the nostalgia I would have expected from such a grand Southern dame. I sensed her eagerness, as if her move would be ending an era. Her response really took me back a bit. Her home, the mansion that had at first held me hostage to the past, was masterfully done and well-appointed. People requested tours to see the inside and to hear the story of Roselawn. It was history! But she said she could leave it tomorrow. Was she was intentionally leaving the past behind? Why had the log cabin been such an important project for her to undertake? Why did she take so much time and provide so much detail about her decision? I was filled with questions, but no verbal answers were forthcoming.

Our talk ended as we reached the back veranda. When she opened the door, the little dog, Summer, was standing there as if she expected us, and we both laughed at her greeting.

My feelings that afternoon were a far cry from those that filled me the very first time I set foot at Roselawn. That first afternoon several years earlier reminded me of all I had encountered and endured while growing up in segregated Glen Allan. Somehow, though, despite the lingering lessons of race and place that continue to surface in my life, spending time at Roselawn with Miss Camille had left me feeling that a different future is indeed possible. We can still remodel as our lives pass through this world. As a baby boomer, I owe this to my country and to the generations of promise—those on our shoulders and those coming after us who will take their cues from the legacy we leave.

Rosabeth Moss Kanter says it best: "A vision is not just a picture of what could be; it is an appeal to our better selves, a call to become something more."

15

Our Shared Reality: The Final Divide

"When we are no longer able to change a situation, we are challenged to change ourselves." —Viktor Frankl

MY STAY AT ROSELAWN WAS COMING TO AN END. I WOULD spend one more night in the mansion, and sleep once more in the white-lace-canopied bed, before giving a morning lecture and heading back home to Oklahoma. While delighted to be going home, I would be leaving with unfinished business—conversations I still wished to have with Miss Camille. By now I had become somewhat accustomed to my quarters, as Miss Camille called my room. Though there was no black butler, I had met Suzy Mor-rell, so unlike the maids or housekeepers I remembered from back home.

My last night went off without incident or tugging at my emotional heartstrings. The plank floor still creaked, but it no longer sounded eerie to me. My room was still magnificent, with plenty of fluffy towels in the bathroom. I was thinking that my circumstances couldn't get much better. Little Cliff was still trying to be guarded, but the adult me was more able to throw caution to the wind. Somewhere during the years of my paths crossing Miss Camille's, I was finding myself not questioning the wisdom and reality of being the guest of this particular plantation owner. I was sensing that a routine was in place—a routine that included me. I was just unable to figure out on my own what had really happened when I met Mrs. Camille Cunningham Sharp.

But that night, with pictures of her newly built log cabin in my head and memories of our visit to Mr. Willie Lee's home continuing to play out, I finally found my nesting place in the bed, and without more emotional conversation to keep me awake, I was soon off to sleep.

I again awoke to South Carolina sunshine directly on my face. The room was awash with sunlight and color, as the crystal chandelier pulled in every hue from the rainbow and sent them throughout the room. Nearly everything those colored lights touched was from another time in history. Though my little routine had been established and I had developed a sense of comfort, being in that particular room still reminded me of a world beyond my reach, of Linden Plantation back home and my very first lesson of "them and us." Even so, I knew where I was and what I had to do. So, without anyone to prod me or any alarm needing to sound twice, I finally un-nestled myself from the sheets, got up, cleaned up, packed my bags, gave my quarters a final look-over and said goodbye to the room that had also hosted a Union general.

That morning as I left the room, I did stop by the small photograph. In the bright sunlight it looked innocent enough, nothing like it did on that night when I felt as if it had assumed a power of suggestion and had pulled me back in time. I just looked at it. I could feel nothing unusual, but the memory from the night was still with me—the night I almost overlooked my kin.

Otherwise, I bumped into no one. Not one servant was in sight as I made my way down the hall to breakfast. When I got to the kitchen, Miss Camille was waiting. The table for two was set. Once again, I shared breakfast with the plantation owner; still no grits, but a great breakfast nonetheless. We sat at the same well-used wooden table. Only Little Cliff recalled that at another place and time I would not have been seated up front and definitely not at the table with the white owner.

From Miss Camille's breakfast table, I again had a panoramic view of her cotton fields, and I was again reminded of their legacy's continued impact upon my life personally and upon America in general. I knew I was not as uneasy as I had been when I first saw Roselawn's cotton fields. Even so, the powerful reminder was always present. Our skin color had not changed. I could not be expected to "just get over it." I'm not sure how many generations that will take. Still, something positive had transpired, and I wanted to fully embrace all that I was sensing. I felt that this experience had been mine for a reason I had yet to understand. I heard Little Cliff's caution, but I also know that over the years of my path crossing with that of Miss Camille's, I was given more hope to continue my pursuit of leaving America better than what I found.

In reality, it was just the two of us going through this experience, not her daughter, Little Camille, or her son, Don. But I realized that they and so many others were looking on. They saw this relationship developing in front of them, and, like me, I am sure they asked no questions. But they saw the signals being sent—signals of promising possibilities.

Our lives send signals. This is the message I want to leave with those to whom I lecture. I want them to fully understand that they are in charge of the signals they send.

I enjoyed my breakfast. The fresh peach jelly was great. Again, Suzy was the only employee there. She knew this was my last day and came into the kitchen to say goodbye. With Miss Camille leading the way and my bags in tow, I made my way down the steep steps arm-in-arm with Miss Camille.

"Suzy, we're off to the college," she politely called back into the house as we made it to the bottom of the steps. I couldn't hear Miss Suzy's response. Maybe she wasn't expected to answer back, and that was just part of their way of living and working together.

As always, Miss Camille was well-dressed and wearing her signature three-inch heels. Carefully, we made our way to her car. I opened the door, threw my stuff in the back and went around to the passenger side to get in. But I hesitated for a moment or two and took another look at the mansion. I was still finding it well out of the ordinary that I had been a guest. I took a long look at the shiny tin roof sparkling in the morning sun. I wanted to remember the wrap-around veranda and the awfully steep steps, which I had learned to master. I took in the flowers emerging from plants over a hundred years old that bordered the mansion. They were unlike any I had seen before. For those few moments, I took it all in with anticipation of seeing it once again. Then I jumped in the car and buckled up. It was time to leave.

Again, it was just the two of us riding together—writing a new chapter in the history of our lives. As she drove from her home, she slowed a bit to point out the log cabin and give me one more opportunity to look at a project of her own design and for her own purpose.

"Clifton, I am so glad I had an opportunity to show you through the cabin. You do like it, don't you?"

I didn't say anything. I smiled. I nodded my head. I was hearing a question that went beyond the look and feel of the cabin itself. Somehow I felt that she was referring to more than the physical place. Maybe this question was more about her own humanity and how she had set out to build equity in her design, starting with the foundation. She had somebody else other than herself in mind. Again, this would have been a great time to embark upon the conversation we never had, the conversation about the lessons of race and place that I'm sure followed both our lives, though she had not experienced all the consequences heaped upon me. Maybe, over the years of our crossings, the pats on the hands had been a code that she trusted I would understand. On some level, I think I did.

From the log cabin, my eyes moved on to the red farm machines making their way down the long cotton rows, like those that had looked so endless when I worked them as a child in the Mississippi Delta. It was backbreaking labor, but with the music of our souls to console us, we survived. As I took in Miss Camille's fields, I really wished that I had spoken to the young black workers we encountered the day before. But they were nowhere to be seen, probably in the cabs of the red tractors, listening to music and hopefully pondering Miss Camille's advice to further their education. I thought about Mr. Willie Lee and wished that his life had turned out differently. And I thought about Don's offer to take a tractor ride with him. I had really wanted that experience. *Next year.*

As we pulled out onto the paved Old Allendale Road, I took one more look back to the tall row of towering oaks guarding Roselawn's dirt lane that seemed to somehow separate the past from the present. I was leaving the Old South and my twentieth century behind and heading back into the real world. I could never have imagined that one speech in Philadelphia could have started one man on a journey to experience so much from the past and to anticipate so much from the future. Although I was leaving Miss Camille's world, I was already making plans to return. A conversation was due both of us.

For a few minutes, we drove squarely into the glare of the morning sun. Although no words were spoken, I felt as if conversation were taking place at some deep, inexplicable level. Today I had no concern that I would be late for my last lecture and then my drive to another college, where I would repeat my talks to another group of South Carolina educators.

Looking out the window, I knew the humidity was rising and that the huge mosquitoes would soon be out, and that no matter how hard I tried, I'd not be able to make cell phone connection until later that night when I got to another city. That's just the way it was in parts of Allendale County.

With nothing to do but think and reflect, I settled back in my seat as Miss Camille drove me through the countryside, leaving cotton fields and peach orchards in the rearview mirror. I was enjoying the drive, the air-conditioned cool, and the quiet.

Without warning, she began slowing down. Miss Camille never slowed down unless she was getting ready to actually stop. Maybe something was wrong. We were nowhere near our destination. True to form, she said not one single word of explanation. Instead, when she carefully pulled off alongside the road, with the motor still running, she looked at me and then pointed across the road. At first, I was unsure of what I was supposed to see. There weren't any peach orchards, no Southern mansion, nor were there any small houses like the home of her old friend, Mr. Willie Lee. Finally, I saw what was right in front of us, a cemetery. She was pointing to the cemetery just across the road.

What was I to say? For a few long, silent moments, we said nothing. The only sounds were those from the motor and the air conditioner.

That early morning and the conversation that ensued is forever etched in my memory. Miss Camille was surprising me again. I could tell that this was the "white cemetery." I could tell that much from the large stately markers, much like those at Greenfield, the white cemetery in Glen Allan. Like most things in Glen Allan while I was growing up, it too was off limits to us, un-less we were cutting or trimming the grass. Greenfield Cemetery was just a place we passed by. There was no reason to stop; we had no relatives there.

Our morning had started out rather simply to get me to the college. So why was I parked right across the road from the final resting place of white Southerners? Were we going to talk? If so, then what would we be talking about? The moments of silence only heightened my sense of the history that followed both our lives. Little Cliff was suddenly was well aware that an older white lady and a black man were parked alongside a rural road. That alone had implications. At that moment, the fact that I had spent the night at the mansion didn't matter. I had just shared breakfast with Miss Camille, and that didn't matter, either.

Finally, Miss Camille broke the silence. "Clifton, we'll just sit here for a moment or two. That's our other home over there, Swallow Savannah. It's a lovely name, isn't it? I love this place." Her eyes squinted as she talked with me. The sun was getting brighter and shining through the trees into her car.

I listened quietly.

"The trees are just wonderful out here. Clifton, look at the shade they make—so many leaves. I just hate it when the leaves fall, but they always do, you know. The leaves always fall. No matter how green and lush they are, they will eventually fall to the ground. But it's so peaceful out here, not like our lives."

As she talked, my nervousness subsided and I found myself caught up in her conversation. Never in my life had I sat across from a cemetery and thought of it as my "other home." I had certainly never sat in a car with a white person across from a white cemetery. I had no reference for what was happening. Even Little Cliff was caught off guard. But I was caught up in her moment—a moment she felt she needed to share with me. Occasionally, she would take her eyes off the cemetery and look directly at me and smile as if I were party to what was in her head. I didn't say anything as she told me who lived where.

"I know many of the people who now rest here. One day, I'll join them."

I listened and the names she called with great familiarity were unfamiliar to me. They were all white. They had lived in South Carolina, not Mississippi. She talked to me as if they were people I knew and cared for. Surely Miss Camille knew that I didn't know these people, and, besides, this was not where black people would have been buried.

Surely she remembered that even in death our segregated world had found ways to continue the social divide. So strict were our rules of social engagement that even at death, we were determined not to cross paths. But it was not so that day. Sitting there on the soft shoulder of a Southern country road, it was as if I were traveling back in time. Unexpectedly and atypically, I sat with her and engaged in conversation about the white cemetery. This was indeed a strange invitation, but Miss Camille had her reasons. I never asked and she never explained. She remembered names and talked about them as if they had just shared supper together yesterday. Obviously, they were people who meant much in her life. Sitting in her black Cadillac, and talking about the end of our days was a moment in time where race, gender and social standing took a back seat to our shared reality—the end of *our* days.

"Clifton, look at all the many markers, addresses, you know," she continued to say, but always stopping so that I could take in all that she was saying. "Some mighty good people are resting there—my husband, Don, among them. I wish you had known him."

Her eyes lit up when she named her husband. It was obvious she loved him and he must have been a good man—one who perhaps shared some of her views about all the people who surrounded his life. If not, why would she have wanted me to know him? I wondered if he would have invited me to spend a few nights in their guest quarters.

"You know, Don was very instrumental in making housing better for African Americans, even bringing indoor toilets into their homes." Interestingly, she looked directly into my eyes when telling me this. I felt as if she wanted to tell me more, take me down more roads in her life. From all I could tell, she was not a spur-of-the-moment lady. I feel as if our sitting across from "Swallow Savannah" was part of a well thought-out plan.

We fell silent, maybe reflecting on our shared, but unequal lives, before she again perked up. She simply repeated what she had said earlier, "People I care about are out there."

I nodded reverently, because I was now thinking about such places in my life, both in Tulsa and the old colored cemetery back home in Glen Allan and how some of the best people from my life were also resting in their quiet places, which I never thought of as their "other home." I could not help thinking about my own daughter, Anne Kathryn, who left us so early in life, when she was just a first-grader, and who now rests underneath the shade of a tree that I didn't intend to plant, in a world like the one we were viewing just across the road. My Annie was buried in what was once an all-white cemetery. My mother, Mary Ester, was also in such a place, now quietly resting by my daughter's side. Miss Camille was right. I, too, knew of such a place where people I still love and care about now call home, Mama Ponk included. The car was filled with emotions emanating from the both of us and in some way reminding us of our shared human journey.

"You know, we have Easter sunrise services here every year, and, Clifton, the sun comes up just right, every time, without fail," she said, her small hands motioning as if her small fingers were the rays of the sun. "Just like now, the rays come right through the trees, making such wonderful trails in the sky, and then they cover everything with God's beauty. When it's time to rest, this will be a good place. Well—in spite of everything—I've had a good life."

I KNEW THE CONVERSATION was over. I could tell by the finality of her closing argument, as it were. She put the car in drive and, looking both ways, slowly pulled back onto the road and made her way to the college. Though our conversation had been rather somber, the spark in her eyes had now returned. She was amazing, even though her life in certain ways represented much of the history of race and place I wanted to forget—even the cemetery that had, like so much else, been designed to remind us of our separate places. Our paths had crossed unexpectedly, and over the course of our times together, I also had experiences that were totally surprising. I found myself looking forward to seeing Miss Camille the following year.

As we drove to the Allendale campus, we talked about the crops and the weather and her excitement about moving from the big house to her log cabin, where she would spend her last days with a friend of her own choosing. Where most people of her standing would relish living their last days surrounded by the artifacts that defined their life, she had opted for something different. She seemed anxious to make the move. It was as if she was leaving yesterday behind and giving herself a fresh new start. I know that we don't have to be paralyzed by the past, no matter how powerful. It isn't always easy, and I also know that. I think she was telling me not to allow the past, no matter how intimidating, to paralyze my future.

With the college in sight, she slowed a bit as she made her way around the perimeter of the campus. As always, she stopped at the main building to let me off. She parked as close as she could for me. It was already hot and muggy, and the mosquitoes were swarming. She didn't turn off the engine. It was too hot to be without the air conditioner. Besides, she was a farmer and had errands to run in town. But she did stay long enough to give me a big hug in the car before she let me out.

She seemed excited over the prospects of my return the next year and I reminded her of our brief conversation about her coming to Tulsa to visit my family and stay in my home and sleep in the bed in our guest room—not one that was once occupied by a Union general. In asking her to be our guest, I was prepared to risk my feelings. She just smiled and said, "We'll see."

With the sun beating down on my head, I stood on the sidewalk and watched until her car was out of sight. Then I made my way into the college where I was greeted by the cool air I so desperately needed. As I quickly closed the big doors to the lobby, I could not help but think about next year and whether or not Miss Camille would be a part of it. The Low Country of South Carolina, this new place to me, had turned out to be so familiar, sending me reeling back and forth from Glen Allan to today, and to many places where I'd stopped in between.

Just off the Old Allendale Road and behind the oak trees covered with Spanish moss was a place that for me fully and completely represented the Old South. In that historic world, my people had been viewed as soulless, suited only to serve those who were considered white. Somehow, though, while growing up in the midst of the Jim Crow segregationist laws, I also experienced the power of community, the "eight habits of the heart" of those who cared for me. Without them I shudder to think the turn of my life. Surprisingly, it was those same habits and their transformative power that garnered me the invitation to Columbia, South Carolina, and subsequently to Allendale, and then to the unexpected hospitality of Roselawn Plantation, where community was forming in new ways.

It was good for me to have passed through Allendale while on my life's journey and to have met Mrs. Camille Cunningham Sharp. For it was also there at Roselawn Plantation, her childhood home, that I bore witness to what could be possible for the generations to come. I could hardly wait for next year and the promise of more discoveries.

We must never lose hope. We must keep faith in tomorrow. It's never too late to be our best selves.

Epilogue

"If you would attain to what you are not yet, you must always be displeased by what you are. For where you are pleased with yourself there you have remained. Keep adding, keep walking, keep advancing." —Saint Augustine

LIFE CHANGED ALL AROUND ME AND WELL-LAID PLANS FELL apart. Due to budget constraints in 2005, I did not return to Allendale; I therefore missed my opportunity to continue my journey with Miss Camille. Unfortunately, during that same year, she fell ill. I wasn't overly concerned. I knew she was very resilient. I knew that our paths would cross again and just maybe I would have the opportunity to get the other half of our story.

It was not to be. In the winter of 2006, she quietly passed away—taking with her the conversations I wanted to hold, but leaving with me the actions of her heart that will long be remembered. When the lessons of race and place show up in my life, as they do, I think of Miss Camille and what is possible. My unplanned and unexpected experiences in Allendale are not to be forgotten. There was so much I wanted to know of her life and how she viewed the world of folks that looked like me. I wanted to know why I had been singled out to walk alongside of her and to be her guest. Conversations I desperately wanted to hold will never be. There are no great revelatory answers to the challenging questions of our paths crossing. All I have are the memories of her actions toward me—walking arm-in-arm down her small hall to my quarters, sharing breakfast together, the gentle pats on the back of my hand, and being chauffeured to visit her friend and the college where I worked. Her actions are forever etched in my memory—a memory that I have gladly shared with you.

I was unable to attend her services, but I wanted to be there, among her family and friends, to share my memories of a lady whose actions could be an example to start America on a conversation about race and place that really matters. I understood from my friend Little Camille that her mother was remembered fondly at the Old Allendale Presbyterian Church, where she had faithfully served, and she was even honored by the State of South Carolina with a period of silence in the legislative chambers. Just as she wished and as she shared with me on our last morning together, she was buried in the cemetery called Swallow Savannah. A "good address," she called it.

The harsh and gentle lessons of race are still with us and I am certainly not the only person shadowed by them. The long reach of racism continues, but so does our opportunity to rid our nation of its virus. To do this, we must forever be vigilant. We must extend invitations to others, even when those invitations might not at first be clearly understood. Viruses do not choose to leave once they have found a comfortable culture in which to live and thrive. This is why I write. This is why I invited you into my thinking, into my fears, into my feelings of intimidation, and to share the hope that I still embrace.

Democracy is not a project. It doesn't have a start and completion date. It is an incredible, continuous process of relationship-building with no end in sight. This means that I can still throw my hat in the ring and seek to make a difference in the world that surrounds me. And so can each of you. It's not too late to invite a neighbor to supper. In her own way, and at the twilight of her life, Miss Camille threw her hat in the ring, and over those several years sought to leave me with a different picture of what could be possible.

On the morning Miss Camille and I sat across from the white cemetery,

I could not know it would be our last time together. Without great speeches and in-depth conversations, with only our genuine understanding of our human journey and the end that comes to all, the irony of life stared us both in the face. The honesty of that morning left me wanting more. For some, who may not be familiar with the social complexity that defines the South, it may be difficult to see what Miss Camille was unraveling and re-weaving. It might be difficult to understand why I didn't insist on a frank conversation of honest truth about our past. I settled for watching and hearing the unspoken as her actions in my presence unraveled and rewove incidents personal to me and yet very familiar to so many others.

As I sat in Miss Camille's car looking across at scores of grave markers, I clearly understood the common ending of our days. We are indeed like blades of grass, here today and gone tomorrow. Even so, the impact of our human presence resonates all over the world. Our presence is known. We build civilizations. We humans marched from caves, and on our way we left towns and cities as proof of our presence. We squared off the land and called ourselves nations. The handprint of our good and greatness is all around us, and so is the handprint of our inhumanity toward others. I have read about the Holocaust. I have sat in the presence of survivors and heard their stories. I have read about the Trail of Tears and talked with Native Americans about their journey of pain and sorrows. I have read about the wars of atrocity in Rwanda and held hands with young people who survived. I have heard their stories firsthand. But I didn't have to read about the horrible residue of slavery upon a people. This is the life I lived in the Mississippi Delta. These are the lingering shadows that follow me. This is the life that came alive on so many fronts while I was a guest at the historic Roselawn Plantation. Realizing the position that South Carolina played in the slave trade, which thousands of Africans passed through, some of whom were my kin, I can better understand why my spirit was so stirred that first day I walked upon the grounds of Roselawn.

I'll never really know why fate allowed me to meet Miss Camille at the twilight of her life, but our paths crossed and our lives touched. I left knowing more clearly that the process continues. Our nation is still maturing, growing and becoming, and as such, courageous unselfish acts must continue to fall like a gentle rain upon the soil of our souls, pushing forth songs of promise and solace. It is complicated like a ball of tangled twine, but if we can but catch that one elusive thread that can change our lives, maybe the next generation and those that follow can unravel more than we dared to dream possible and in the process weave a new tapestry reflecting more of what we all share in common—our gift of humanity.

Though the life of our nation at times is still burdened by the legacy of slavery, I will do my part to ensure that the Jim Crow laws and mentality I knew as a child do not find new and even more vicious ways to show up in our lives. Viruses must be exterminated, as well as their breeding grounds. If not, they will show up again.

As for me, I know I owe this to Marshall, my son. I will not shut down. I will not become paralyzed by the lingering lessons of race and place. They still show up in our workplaces and on playgrounds. They show up in public parks and private places. They show up in fast-moving cars whose occupants speak vile words with their fingers. They show up in courtrooms and in classrooms. They sneak into our places of worship and into our colleges and universities. Even so, I will not shut down to what is possible. When anger swells inside of me, I will remember one particular plantation owner and her small pats on the back of my hand. I will remember the last days spent with Miss Camille. I will deal with racial bigotry as best I can—with the days at Roselawn to remind me of what is possible and Miss Camille's arm in mine. That memory keeps me encouraged to believe that the impossible is possible—bridges can be built. And it's never too late to do so. The reality of those oftentimes challenging feelings will continue motivating me to embrace the remodeling task that is set before my generation. We must create safe harbors, welcoming front porches where respect, affirmation and inclusion are the daily fare and not just a distant dream. We must find our ways of extending invitations for others to walk through dimly lit hallways in unfamiliar places, to understand the reality of the past.

This is my invitation to you. Extend your hand across the barriers of the past. Such courage is needed if we are to walk into a future with promising possibilities for all.

～